MW00324219

"**Lumari's book really a**
The exquisite channeled k.
comes to us at just the right time as it reveals how we can
directly access the Divine to not only uplift our own lives but
all of humanity. Moreover, whenever I sat to read, I felt a sweet
flow of healing energy throughout my body. This is not just a
book - it's a life-changing experience."

~ Debra Poneman
Founder / CEO, Yes to Success, Inc.

"**A remarkably timely book for evolving consciousness.**
Lumari takes the readers on a multi-dimensional journey
to reveal the hidden Streams Of Consciousness that have
been awakening, inspiring and guiding humanity since our
earthy beginnings. Each exploration of the twelve streams she
offers, each sacred practice and calling forth that she shares
is an awakening mindful journey through the wisdom of the
universe, the soul of being, and the heart of all consciousness.
What a gift to all of us!"

~ Dr. Sue Morter
Author of #1 International Best Selling book The Energy Codes:
The 7-Step System to Awaken Your Spirit, Heal Your Body,
and Live Your Best Life

"**Tap into your higher spiritual self**
In Lumari's book, Streams of Consciousness, you are taken
on a journey that allows you to tap into your higher spiritual
self. You'll learn to align yourself with the frequencies of the
twelve streams of consciousness gaining greater awareness
and a spiritual understanding of who you really are. The
journey is about opening up your heart, mind and spirit to
the possibilities that life has to offer.

~ David Riklan,
Founder – SelfGrowth.com

"**An entrancing read. It will change your life.**
Lumari's extraordinary book begins with a deep insight - that a singular emanation from the Mysterious Source that calls itself Alawashka is the source of creation and encompasses all consciousness and at every level of existence, elemental, physical and spiritual. It exists everywhere and within everything, and Lumari's relationship with Alawashka has allowed them to create this book, Streams of Consciousness, together. They are to be commended as they have created very good medicine indeed."

~ Hank Wesselman PhD.
Anthropologist, Shamanist Teacher, and Award-winning Author

"**Sharing this ancient and contemporary wisdom with the world**
This book tells the story and reveals how the Streams of Consciousness, twelve ancient and contemporary vibrations on our planet. These clear, high-frequency, spiritual energy fields exist to guide us and society to our connection with the Divine. Lumari channels "The Original Language" to speak clearly through her and presents the highest vibrations with wonderful understanding, special practices and blessings that create awakenings. Streams of Consciousness is a book of the highest quality and vibration.

Thank you Lumari, for being a guiding light on my Akashic Journey and for sharing this new and unique wisdom with the world."

~ Lisa Barnett
International Bestselling Author and Founder of Akashic Knowing School of Wisdom

"**Truly revolutionary, enlightening and inspiring**
Lumari's resonance and brilliance shines through in her divinely inspired latest book. She is incredible at revealing the frequencies of creation activating the expansion of consciousness that is currently happening for humanity. Unveiling the once-secret Streams of Consciousness, now we

have access to these illuminating frequencies, teachings and a direct connection to the Divine. The gifts and accelerated practices that she shares are true higher teachings.

Lumari is a gift and Streams of Consciousness is the blessing to you the reader. "

~ Gary Stuart
International bestselling Author, Speaker, Master
Constellation healing facilitator

"A Life-Changing book
This is a transformational book that we all need right now. You will discover the hidden secrets of the twelve Streams Of Consciousness and how to recognize, understand and access their messages, energies, and inspiring qualities. This is a beautiful well-written book with love & light...very relatable, comforting, and uplifting. Lumari brings you on a mind-altering, heart-opening, awakening journey into the cosmos, your divine nature, and our world.

The magic, spirit, and revelation in this book illuminate the clear, high-frequency, spiritual energy fields that exist to guide us and society to our connection with the Divine. See how your heart's soul purpose resonates with the Streams Of Consciousness. I definitely recommend reading Lumari's Streams of Consciousness book! You will be so glad you did!"

~ Sylvia Moss
Vibrational, Sound Healer, Channel, and author of Angels of New York, a meditative photographic journey

"I can't recommend this book enough!
Streams of Consciousness isn't simply a spiritual book. It's an evolutionary energy source that shifts your vibration just by being in contact with the words. It raises your energy frequencies and connects you more deeply to the divine. I could feel the powerful transmissions of the words and the fine attunements happening as I was reading the sacred words

in each chapter. If you are on a conscious path of evolution the Streams of Consciousness is a profound source of wisdom, guidance and transformational vibrational tools that you must have. Just opening up and reading the words within will alter you and have an immediate impact. I will add this book as a new tool in my repertoire to keep my vibration high."

~ Debbie Lynn Grace
Author, Transformational Leader, International speaker,
Intuitive

"I am forever changed and grateful.
Streams of Conscious is more than the written word of Alawashka, the vibrational source of creation. It is an activation into the twelve ancient pathways to the Divine. Each stream brought me into a deeper relationship to this Outpouring of Divine Energy."

~ John Nelson
Author The Magic Mirror, COVR winner Best Book

"An avenue toward enlightenment
With a brilliance equal to the to the great visionaries, Lumari has masterfully channeled a hidden vibrational language and has presented its mystery in the Streams of Consciousness. Lumari is a modern sage who has much to offer anyone who seeks their higher calling. This work will reward those who explore her fresh metaphysical insights."

~ D.S. Lliteras
Author of internationally acclaimed spiritual novels.

"This is a powerful and experiential book, for spiritual awakening and the contemporary renaissance of humanity. Lumari provides all the healing anyone ever wanted in one valuable book. This is a timely experience for everyone, everywhere. Let it be you."

~ Louise M. Mitchell (Laughing Waters)
Author-Contemporary Shaman, Author, Speaker and Facilitator

STREAMS OF CONSCIOUSNESS

STREAMS OF CONSCIOUSNESS

Discover the Twelve Hidden Frequencies of Creation.
Activate your Higher Calling and Uplift Our World.

LUMARI

an Alawashka® book

BLUE
STAR

For information on licensing or special sales, please contact Lumari at sales@BlueStarNerwork.com.

Trade Paperback ISBN: 978-0-9993259-3-3

Printed in the United States of America
Book Design and Cover Art: Lumari

Published by Blue Star
BLUE STAR NETWORK
7 Avenida Vista Grande, Santa Fe, New Mexico 87508

LUMARI
www.Lumari.com

Printed in the United States of America

DEDICATION:

I dedicate this book to all of you,
to the thousands students who have participated in
my Alawashka gatherings and trainings,
to my dear clients who celebrate life and wisdom,
and to the light-bringers, illuminators and healers
who have read my books,
joined my meditations and
who have come to this life to share their gifts

My appreciation, wonder and blessings.

Contents

FOREWARD   i

ACKNOWLEDGEMENTS   v

OUR OPENING:
A Message From Lumari   7

PREFACE:
Our Invitation   9

INTRODUCTION:
A Message from Alawashka   15

PART 1
Invitation   19
Sacred Teachings and Attunements

CHAPTER ONE:
The Singular Outpouring   21
Celestial Pathways of Divine Connections

CHAPTER TWO:
Within the Streams   31
Choosing to Experience the Streams of Consciousness

CHAPTER THREE:
Revelations and Requests   39
Honoring the Masters and Guardians of the Streams

CHAPTER FOUR:
Personal Participation   45
Ways to Approach these Sacred Frequencies

PART 2
Initiation   59
The Twelve Streams of Consciousness

CHAPTER FIVE:
The Stream of Purity   61
Clear, Awakening and Pure Frequencies of Divine light.

CHAPTER SIX:
The Stream of Honor   71
Recognition and Appreciation of the Divine in All Things

CHAPTER SEVEN:
The Stream of Compassion   79
Universal Deep Heart Awakening and Kinship

CHAPTER EIGHT:
The Stream of Neutrality   87
Open-minded Wisdom of the Divine in the All.

CHAPTER NINE:
The Stream of Harmony   97
Multi-Focused Interplayful Collaboration and Synchronicity

CHAPTER TEN:
The Stream of Beauty and Grace   105
Gifts of Universal Love, Inspiration and Self-expression

CHAPTER ELEVEN:
The Stream of Wisdom   113
Infinite Understanding, Recognition and Presence

CHAPTER TWELVE:
The Stream of Truth   125
Revelations of Divine Light and Absolute Knowing

CHAPTER THIRTEEN:
The Stream of Radiance   135
Transmission of Wisdom, Knowing, Illumination and Connectivity

CHAPTER FOURTEEN:
The Stream of Reciprocity   145
Generous and Abundant Relationships and Interconnection of All

CHAPTER FIFTEEN:
The Stream of Universality   157
Pervasive, Unlimited Divine Presence in Everything and Everyone

CHAPTER SIXTEEN:
The Stream of Unity   165
Foundation of Peace and Oneness

CHAPTER SEVENTEEN:
A Calling Forth   175
Realize your Personal Harmonious Resonance

CHAPTER EIGHTEEN:
Entering the Stream   179
Begin your Relationship in a Blessed Way

PART 3
Invocation   185
Calling Forth and Entering a Stream

CHAPTER NINETEEN:
Invocations and Practices   187
Dancing in the Streams

PART 4
Inspiration   247
Opening the Way

CHAPTER TWENTY:
Engaging The Streams   249
Gain a Deeper Understanding with a Stream

CHAPTER TWENTY ONE:
Influences of The Streams   255
Transformation and Shaping of Global Perception

CHAPTER TWENTY TWO:
The New Illuminated Paradigm   263
Creating a New World Reality

About The Author   273

FOREWARD:
by Maureen St. Germain

Lumari's book, Streams of Consciousness is exquisite. It is one of the many ways to become fifth dimensional. Attracting these very high frequency streams into your life will cause you, the reader, very likely to shift and change dramatically. In this beautifully written narrative, Alawashka, channeled through Lumari, illuminates the creation of these energies and their very high expression in creation.

It may be a new concept for you, as there are many hidden mysteries in creation, yet Lumari lays out a very detailed account of how these streams of consciousness came to be, their very high frequencies and how you may access them. She tells how they were constructed, and how you may claim them for yourself. Just holding the book in your hands may cause you to "remember these frequencies."

Much can be said about discovering our true lineage. You may not have heard of Alawashka but their energy is real, and you are about to embark upon an amazing journey. This journey is unlike anything you have ever undertaken. It is a journey of discovery of the amazing Streams of Consciousness, more like RIVERS. Immerse yourself into them and you will be forever changed.

You are offered a very real, deep understanding of how these energies came to exist along with detailed instructions on how you may access them. You are guided by this information every step of the way. Each "stream" is defined with love, care and authenticity. You can experience these organizing principles yourself. You may discover that they have already served you. You may resonate with one, several or all of them.

Even if you have never accessed these energies (doubtful) you will begin to recognize them. Their familiarity will take you by surprise. At the same time, your evolution can be given a jump start at remembering, reverently, their power and influence you may bring into your life. I fully believe this information was seeded into the reality through Lumari as very high vibrational souls came into embodiment, so they would have a template and directions to stay on track, and to stay the course.

There are so many separate energies that have become available to humanity at this time, there is no reason to fail. This book will particularly appeal to those whose lineage is beyond this galaxy and are very likely from source directly. There are quite a few of us out on the planet. You may be one of them.

As I read this book I began to notice that I have embodied these streams, expressing these energies for quite some time. You may have too! They were quite familiar. You will begin to discover that so much you already know is coming to you from the streams of consciousness, albeit unawares.

Now instead of accessing them by default, you can access them by design. In addition, because this book so well defines each layer of expression of these twelve Streams of Consciousness you now have a map that will take you where-ever you wish to go in this vast unfolding universe. Now is the time to awaken to their power, universality and authentic expression through you.

Although these secrets have been closely held for eons, you now have full access and approval from these amazing beings that embody the Streams of Consciousness. You can expect a remarkable experience from taking the step to embody them for yourself.

As an author and channel, Lumari has access to the highest hidden wisdom available in our times. She embodies these "Streams of Consciousness" with clarity, authenticity and compassion. She explains them with loving patience, detailing every step, answering with great detail, to the point that these "Streams of Consciousness" are irresistible. But that's not all, Lumari goes on to provide specific ceremonies where you may access these mighty Streams of Consciousness for yourself! It is my deep pleasure to support this work and encourage you to read and apply all that is within.

Maureen St. Germain is a Mystic, and Akashic Records Guides Founder. She teaches Ascension awareness tools globally resulting in empowerment and transformation of individuals and organizations. She is the author of, Waking Up in 5D, voted the best-selling book in America by Independent retailers and winner of the Bronze COVR award in 2018.

Awaken, Access and Celebrate
higher levels of your Soul Calling

STEP 1 – START HERE

Thank you for purchasing Streams Of Consciousness, a book
that can truly change your life.

As a thank you for purchasing my book, I am providing several
bonus items to enhance your experience and enable you to
make great progress with your spiritual journey.

Take 1 minute and download your personal Activations Journal,
a companion journal to this book and receive more free gifts, too.

Discover more about the Invocations Audio Course, Streams Of
Consciousness workshops and private coaching with Lumari
and Create and Live your Bigger Vision.

To receive your free gifts go to www.CosmicStreams.com

STEP 1 – Download your gifts and start reading
at www.CosmicStreams.com

Acknowledgements

In deepest thanks to the Goddess and Alawashka who bring the clear voice of great Divine and open the gateways of wisdom and illumination. I am honored to activate, teach and share healing through the Frequencies of Creation.

Gratitude and appreciation to the Keepers of Divine Expression, the Akashic Records, who have always guided my knowing.

Profound appreciation to the Great Beings and the Masters of the Streams of Consciousness, who asked that I reveal their existence now and who continue to inspire me to share the gifts I receive and share their voices with you.

In sacred gratitude to my beloved husband Peter whose deep unwavering love is beyond words as we travel through the Cosmic All together. You make my heart dance, my creativity soar, my eyes smile and make me laugh out loud every day.

To Lyz Meyer, my dearest friend, appreciation for our lifetimes of friendship and for your help in the editing and proofreading this book.

Special gratitude to Maureen St Germain for her thoughtful contribution and writing the foreward to this book. I truly appreciate her friendship, wisdom and high vibrations. She truly lights a path for all.

OUR OPENING:

A Message From Lumari

Thank you for being here.

I am honored and inspired to share this book with you and reveal the Streams of Consciousness and these light-filled frequencies, so you can recognize and explore their majesty. I received and channeled this book over 10 years ago and was told to wait until the time was right. Now, is the time.

In this book, I'm channeling Alawashka, the Original Language and Vibrational Source of Creation and bringing through the creation frequencies, wisdom and teachings. We have a unique, sacred relationship and I am honored in this.

When I received and channeled this book, the flows of Divine moved me to reveal secrets most of us didn't know. I opened to receive the knowledge, messages and blessings, with the understanding that some day, you would have them, too. I love being a vehicle of wisdom and bringing this wisdom to you. The revelations in this book are evolutionary and transformational. They can open your own energy fields and perceptions about what inspires, moves and delights your soul.

This book, Streams Of Consciousness, reveals and introduces you to the unknown vibrational pathways of divine flow that have blessed our planet since ancient times. It is also is a journey within those vibrational Streams. I invite you and we invite you to take this journey of discovery and celebrate your soul, your being and your connection with the Divine. I'm honored to share it and we will be having gatherings, trainings and group participation for you to experience these Streams Of Consciousness in a more dedicated way.

Channeling this book is a fluid and creative collaboration with Alawashka. I am listening for the words, images and frequencies, being shared and I am translating the forms, images and visions I am shown and perceive. I am flowing with many different energies and multi-dimensional concepts, while I am having conversations and discussions with Alawashka and other beings that become part of this book. Channeling this book is a dance of listening, creating and participating. As I dipped into this book again, even more mysteries were revealed. Naturally, I have written all of the words, and also they are flowing to me and through from the Heart of the Universe.

I have also added a poem for each Stream Of Consciousness. It's written in my voice and included at the beginning of the chapter for each Stream. The poem is an alignment for you.

Thank you for being here. Thank you for the gifts you bring and your openness to discover the blessings from beyond!

Blessings

May your journey be a blessing
that shines in beauty,
love and sacred participation that
uplifts your life and our world.

Many blessings,
Lumari

PREFACE

Our Invitation

This is our formal invitation. We invite you to discover
the blessings, wisdom and vibrations of The Streams
of Consciousness. We are revealing these hidden
vibrations, so that you can more fully participate in the Divine
All, for your own being and for the awakening of humanity.
Our invitation to you is to open yourself, your heart, mind
and spirit to the vibrations of The Streams of Consciousness,
so you may experience these blessings.

We invite you to approach these beautiful revelations
and openings with Honor, Love and Truth. Think of this as
an invitation to a formal event, so you know it's important
to RSVP. Your RSVP means that you are open to hold
these secrets and teachings as sacred and that you treat
this wisdom and these revelations in the highest manner
possible. Take a deep breath. Please inwardly RSVP.

We reveal the secrets and hidden vibrations of The
Streams of Consciousness to you. In this we create a clear
sacred pathway, so the wisdom, frequencies, teachings
and revelations can flow unhindered to you now. This is a
tremendous undertaking and has required us to confer with
many Divine Beings to clear the way for this to happen and
to happen now.

There is a deep respect for the essence and ways of
all beings as we reveal these secrets and their unknown
vibrational pathways. While I, Alawashka, can reveal as
I wish, I have asked all the beings and masters involved

with The Streams of Consciousness for their permission and blessing. Lumari has done the same. We honor, appreciate and are grateful for these beings, their wisdom and our sacred stance reveals that to them. They know we will reveal these invisible influences in the highest expression.

We also asked if they had any special requests of us in this doing. The requests of another being, in how to be treated or to use the wisdom they hold and create, is honored and understood. This shows deep respect and appreciation.

This is a sacred teaching, Honor, Love and Truth. Lumari and I teach that Honor, Love and Truth are the three most important qualities or principles for being.

Honor comes first. If the qualities of Honor are not present, then Love is not available, and Truth becomes a weapon. When Honor is present, Love proceeds as an acknowledgment and relatedness of the Divine, and Truth is a beacon of light, spirit and awakening. What is honor? It is a reverence, a level of attention and focus that holds respect and appreciation. It is clear recognition, regard and confirmation for the energies, beings, life, wisdom and wholeness set forth. It is also a declaration of that respect, appreciation and acknowledgment. Honor resonates to the pinnacle of vibrations.

The highest spiritual work takes a person and being dedicated to honoring and seeing all of the ramifications of his or her thoughts, intentions and actions in a matter. As you reach toward new wisdom or communication, you hold the utmost respect for the life, the path and the essence of all beings and circumstances related to their personal explorations.

We begin the introduction of this book with teachings and explanations about Honor, Love and Truth, because by being able to discern levels of Honor, Love and Truth as ways of living and as frequencies, you will be able to travel within and hold higher levels of spirituality and personal awakening. When you are able to hold these energies of

Honor, Love and Truth and when others are also able to do so, then the energies of enlightenment that each person is praying for, will more easily come into viability. Your lives will shift into higher energies and the new creation will be much more easily accessible to your life and your world.

This is channeled and collaborative information. While you may have read other channeled works, for Lumari, channeling my being and wisdom is a collaborative event. We bring it forth together. We have a deep relationship in which the wisdom of my being is transferred into her own being. We have been in this relationship for longer than either of us care to discuss. I ask, that each of you honor and appreciate this special relationship for the grace and glory of All.

I use the example of my relationship with Lumari, so it will help you know how to relate to other similar situations in your own life. In your own path to awakening, you will want a deeper understanding of how to relate to information from others, how to hold your own personal experiences and how to relate to each other.

Please Honor yourself. Honor your heart and being. Honor your brilliance. Honor your choice to be within this book and these secret teachings. The honor you have will be extended to you. As each person grows to honor and acknowledge and respect each other and each other's wisdoms, ways and gifts, then greater joy and fulfillment will flow on this planet and in your hearts. You will feel Love and know and speak Truth.

In this book you will be exploring your connections to the Streams of Consciousness. I reveal the teachings of honor through these examples, so you will know how to approach specific streams, if you so choose. Give Honor, Love and Truth to yourself. If you connect with one Stream of Consciousness and it excites you, then read about It and feel it. If you connect with one Stream of Consciousness and you do not feel it or it doesn't feel right at the moment, Honor your Self, give yourself Love and follow that Truth.

To accord and uphold honor, brings honor to you. In this state of recognition, you resonate to the energies of honor and your own vibrational pattern is uplifted. When you feel the honor and extend the honor, you are upholding the frequency of honor and thusly, allowing it to spread. It may or may not mean that you will always receive honor in return, because the teachings and practice of honor are not constantly evident in your world. It does mean that you personally can live in honor and expand your resonance of honor. You will be able to distinguish honor. You will be more and more able to extend honor and thereby, your own vibrational pattern will become more and more clear, illuminated and awakened to the highest and deepest levels of spirit.

These are important sacred teachings. We, Lumari and I, share these sacred teachings and hidden mysteries with you with honor for your life and your spiritual journey. Knowing the protocols, knowing how to approach and connect with all beings from a place of honor, smooths the way for the most elegant of spiritual experiences. It holds your own energy and soul being in a higher perspective and frequency, which gives you a greater clarity. As you learn to hold and express your honor toward other aspects of spirituality, your respect for your own life and being will grow and you will graciously expand into higher spiritual realms. We honor you with our words and blessings. You honor us with your presence in this moment. It is a blessing for all.

Are you ready to RSVP? Your RSVP means that you are open to hold these secrets as sacred and that you treat this wisdom and these revelations in the highest manner possible. Your RSVP means that you will listen to your inner guidance and experience these frequencies and teachings in the highest manner possible for yourself.

Please accept our invitation to the Streams of Consciousness and inwardly RSVP.

Blessings

May your wisdom expand
in grace and delightful recognition.
May each teaching and knowing on your path
contribute to your joy, awakening and beauty.

INTRODUCTION

A Message from Alawashka

I am Alawashka, the Original Language and Vibrational Source of Creation. Through my being this book unfolds. If you have read Lumari's other books, listened to her music and attended her events and teachings, then you will know of me. I am also speaking with you now, to bring these most blessed frequencies and revelations to light. In my fullness, creation is activated and flows through me. Lumari is my channel and sole/soul voice of my being, the breath of my breath, and always will be the clearest channel of my words. She brings this awakening wisdom and frequencies to this world.

This book is channeled, which means that Lumari speaks my words for me. She brings the frequencies to light and to life. We, Lumari and myself, are revealing and introducing you to the twelve Streams of Consciousness that were created for your blessing. The Masters of the Streams of Consciousness, who were instrumental in creating the streams, also contribute to this book and these sacred energies.

This book, Streams of Consciousness, reveals upper level secret wisdom that has been long unknown and untold and introduces you to the mysteries of the twelve Streams of Consciousness existing on this planet. In this book, Streams of Consciousness, are many revelations, attunements and awakenings. Hidden mysteries are revealed, patterns are shifted and new insights and Divine connections form. When you read this book, know there are expansive frequencies held in the words, in the pages, in the opening and even as you hold this book. These are now here for you to receive.

As you read this book, you may feel energies flowing with you and through you. You may notice clearing, healing, enlightening energies that create new perspectives in your life and presence. This book, Streams of Consciousness, reveals the wisdom that has been hidden and also contains clear energies, so if you wish to connect on many levels, you will have the opportunity to do so.

Hidden Mysteries

The Streams of Consciousness are the unknown and long forgotten avenues of spiritual energy and participation that were created for humanity by Great Beings. We reveal this hidden knowledge to bless and align this planet and the lives and futures of all humanity and beings sharing this reality. We share these wisdoms, because it is time for you to know more of how this world is organized and what other avenues of delight and appreciation are open to your spiritual participation. It is time for you to have clear choices in your spiritual illumination.

Once a secret and ancient knowledge is revealed, it cannot be conveniently hidden again. Therefore, please understand that what we are revealing is truly untold and this wisdom is held within the highest esteem by many enlightened masters and illuminated beings. We are revealing the long held hidden vibrations of the Streams of Consciousness, so you can access the beauty of any stream and travel into the Divine wholeness from that unique perspective.

The Streams of Consciousness are clear, vibrational, spiritual trails of energy that bring you continual, direct access to the Divine. They have existed since the most ancient times. They are created for humanity to open your view and present an invitation to experiences of Divine knowing, presence and illumination in more focused vibrational pathways.

We write this book, reveal these secrets and share these frequencies to open the sacred pathways, so you may receive the expanded blessings that were created for you and that are open for you. You are awakening. You are opening to the higher wisdoms and dimensions. Now, we reveal the Streams of Consciousness, so you may experience higher realms that resonate on Gaia Terra, your Earth. The Streams of Consciousness hold specialized and attuned frequencies and bring sacred energies to you and your world for your own enlightenment, blessing, awakening, inspiration and consciousness. We use all of these words, because your own blessed pathway in these frequencies will be your own choice and experience of the Divine One and All.

We will reveal how and why the Streams of Consciousness were created and developed and how you may gain access to their sacred energies, knowings and vibration. Each Stream of Consciousness has a special attunement, vibrational acceleration and focus that opens pathways for you to have direct contact with the Divine. These unique vibrations are now also held within this book. You may feel and sense them, now. The words, patterns and messages of the Streams of Consciousness are active herein.

This book is a collaborative, channeling, spiritual event. Lumari is the author and channel bringing these frequencies, wisdom and teachings to you. I am Alawashka, the Original Language and Vibrational Source of Creation. Lumari is my channel and reveals this hidden matrix to you.

We, Lumari and Alawashka, are revealing and introducing you to the twelve Streams of Consciousness that were created for your blessing in ancient times and are still connected and active on your planet, Gaia Terra, now. The Masters of the Streams of Consciousness also contribute to this book and these sacred energies.

Now, we introduce you to the mysteries of the twelve Streams of Consciousness.

As a special gift for you, I have created the Streams Of Consciousness Activations Journal.
This journal is a powerful companion that will guide you on your journey in this book. You will gain greater insights, healing and awakening as you create your direct, personal connection to the Divine.

Gain a richer experience of the Streams and download your free Streams Of Consciousness Activations Journal and more free gifts at www.CosmicStreams.com

Blessings

A Blessing from Alawashka

May you continue to embrace, experience and share
your beauty, awakening and vision,
while growing in your own being
as an enlightening presence.

PART 1
Invitation

Sacred Teachings and Attunements

CHAPTER ONE:

The Singular Outpouring

A singular outpouring of Divine energy encompasses all consciousness. It is pure radiant energy. It is a real, although symbolic, illumination of the Divine who is available in all things, in all times and in all places. This vast outpouring of Divine energy that includes light and sound and the thoroughly intangible essence of awareness moves through all of nature, through all universes and all minute particles. It is as if an immense, yet invisible central sun is beaming light in every direction, continuously, forever. This singular illuminating energy is all pervasive. It effortlessly flows through, around and within all things. There is no separation from the Divine energy and awareness. In the vast expanses of its connection with all that is and will be, it is intimate. This singular outpouring of Divine energy reaches through all creation and supports all creation. It permeates every aspect of the All. This singular outpouring may also be called the unified field.

As we speak of creation, know that I am Alawashka, the Original Language and Vibrational Source of Creation. I am the consciousness through which creation takes place.

Creation moves from me and through me into all worlds and this world. As we speak about the Streams of Consciousness, as I describe the Masters and Guardians of the Streams of Consciousness, know that their creation flows through me into the wholeness and beyond.

In this wholeness, this singular outpouring, this unified field, all exists. Every particle and every being exists within the wholeness of the Universal All. Through this remarkable unity, many individual things are created and live. Within the unity are galaxies, star systems, planets, beings, humans, animals, plants and many other forms of consciousness. Each consciousness, each particle has a life inside the wholeness. Humans co-exist with nebulae. Photons co-exist with star beings.

   The chronology of awareness is endless. Creation unfolds. Life and consciousness desire to move into the fullness of their expression. This impetus initiates growth, exploration and expansion. In more ancient times, all life flowed within the singular outpouring. While each individual being had a unique perspective and life, all flowed within the Singular Outpouring. All were aware of each other and consciousness was a singular event.

The Inception of the Streams of Consciousness

In the ancient and distant past, while a group of beings were exploring the wholeness, they moved into a vibration that is best described as concentration. As they concentrated, their focus narrowed and became more intensified as it did. The narrowing of their focus, their accentuated concentration, was profound and exhilarating. In their delight, these beings continued to compress their attention. Where once they would perceive clusters of galaxies moving in a vast ballet, they began to center their attention upon one section of the galaxy. They could feel the shift of awareness between the all-encompassing vastness and the compression of their concentration. The realization that these seemingly separate focuses could exist and be experienced was electrifying for them. As they began to refine and narrow their focus, they began to experience more specific energies and resonances. The singular attention gave way to many different experiences and focuses. With exhilaration, they immersed themselves in ever more compressed views and experiences within the All.

Life gathers and moves energy. The intense concentration of these Great Beings gathered energy along the path of their focus. As their individual focus narrowed, they generated pathways related to their concentration. The beings themselves did not compress energy, nor did the objects of their attention. The energy of their attention consolidated. Their intense focus created a gathering of energy that corresponded with the subject of their attention. The power of their keen focus created a resonance with what they were focused on and this combination created a beam of energy with the qualities of their experience. When they were concentrating on a particular star, filling themselves with the roiling aspects of the fiery gases, they noticed that the space connecting them with that star absorbed that quality. The space pulsed with the fiery excitement of a star in a cycle of explosion. Their own attention and the qualities of the star created a resonance. Energy converged and consolidated between the beings and the star, because of their intense, individualized focus. In all of the vastness of their lives, they had never experienced the richness of this moment. It was a quickening.

These Great Beings then proceeded to focus on the space between themselves and their subject. They observed energies and then compressed them. This was another revelation. With their concentrated focus, they absorbed qualities from all areas of the universe and assembled them into experiential vibrations. They delighted in this new wonder. They blended their experiences and observations of other consciousnesses, planets and life and narrowed their focus to create spaces where those collective qualities would exist. They generated localized events formed from their intense focus and the qualities of their chosen subject. Their focus, the qualities of their focus subject and the spaces where those qualities converged and existed became trails of energy within the Singular Outpouring of the Divine.

Trails of energy were created when these Great Beings began to move their all-encompassing focus, inclusive of the Divine, into a focus of more individual experience. The focus of more individual experience allowed them to hold the Divine Oneness and also have a unique experience from the all-encompassing. In this way, they explored new ways of experiencing and creating in the universe. The Divine was always present within them, and they could loosen that focus and experience awareness in a more individual fashion. The totality of the Divine was with them and they could narrow their attention to a more localized event or experience. These grand and Great Beings were exhilarated by the opportunity to explore consciousness in a more intimate manner. They could enter into a relatedness that was penetrating and singular and intense in a different manner than the all-encompassing flow of Divine essence. These Great Beings experienced a more individual focus, and were never separated from the Divine All. There was not a moment when they felt apart from the All and the One. They did not focus on the individual to separate from the Divine or eliminate or isolate anything or anyone or any experience. This individualized focus thrilled them. It was an avenue of creation, an avenue of intense vibrational focus and delight.

As these Great Beings did this, they eventually decided to work with the Divine to create special streams of energy as guidance systems. The trails were like reminders of energy. As guidance systems, they contained very precise properties that would guide another being to a particular destination and experience. As reminders, the trails held qualities and energies that would engage another in very profound and intimate experiences. The trails can be thought of as a beacon or as a shower. An individual essence, a grand being or a collective of consciousness, could be off in the universe creating and then tune into the trail and replenish their essence or use it to return to their preferred location of origin and awareness. They could return home, to their world, galaxy, collective awareness or preferred place in the All by connecting with this trail and precise focus. They could also follow the trail into the encompassing embrace of the Divine and radiate with renewed awakening and wisdom and connection.

Through the bliss and delight of the Great Beings' creation, and by their own individual experience, each and every being could dip into the trails and awaken and infuse themselves with a stronger energy of all unification Goddess essence. The individualized focus and resonance created a few, specific trails of profound illumination and wonder. These are the Original Streams of Consciousness.

The Original Streams of Consciousness have been in existence for billions of years. Yet they were not always there, nor did they need to be there. A person or being does not need the Streams of Consciousness to remember, connect with or become infused with Divine energy. The streams were like beacons of light, attuned to a realm of participation for the Great Beings. They pointed to the Divine energy to make it easier to lock into this unique energy experience.

The energy of the Divine is present within everything and everyone. The Great Beings knew this. They did not create the streams, because they were afraid of forgetting their Divine connection. They did not create the streams, because they were lost. They created the streams, because they thought it was a wonderful reminder and an efficient way of connecting. They used them as signs and markers. You could think of them as neon signs on a long stretch of highway. The signs made it clear and easy to find a localized vortex of purified energy to dip into, renew connection and bask in the energies of the Divine All.

Many beings did not use the Original Streams of Consciousness at all. They chose to be in Singular

Outpouring. Some beings preferred the Original Streams of Consciousness. It is so with many things. The way of creation is often designed by preference. A particular focus is preferred by certain beings, and not preferred by others. Each being creates through their preferred focus.

Later in time, the Original Streams of Consciousness were used for other purposes, as well. They were used to remind beings of their location and help them return home. This means that when a being, ensconced in their individual focus, was traveling multi-dimensionally and exploring far from their preferred location of being, the stream of energy could be tuned into and guide them toward their home location. The Original Streams of Consciousness were used to frame a particular reference.

As individual focus developed, many beings tuned or adapted their streams to enhance particular collections of energy that they delighted in and preferred. All of the stream was attuned to the Divine. Nothing was separated or distorted. Every Stream of Consciousness is a direct link to the Divine One. Yet, some beings preferred a stream to the Silence Of The All. When they adapted their own stream, they tuned it to their preference.

So, if a being preferred the Silence Of The All, their stream would attune them first, to this blessed silence and the qualities generated by this silence. They would awaken to the grand quietude of being and replenish their awareness within this space. The stream they preferred would be one of silence. Other beings preferred the chaos of creation. They adored the churning nature of life in continual reorganization. They delighted in feeling the endless flow of all life participating in the frenzy of attraction. These beings attuned their stream to provide them with this experience of the Divine.

In this fashion, the Original Streams of Consciousness created by the Great Beings, some of whom became the Masters of the

Streams, were adapted to the preferences of those who used them. All is perfect in this.

The Original Streams of Consciousness were then adapted to the needs or wishes of those beings and collectives that used them. They were tuned to certain energies or qualities of the Divine. These streams always had a full connection to the Great All, to the Divine, the Goddess, the Singular Outpouring. No being ever felt isolated from the All while experiencing the stream. No being ever felt isolated from the All from within their awareness. It is that one being would prefer to experience the All through the unique focus of a stream.

There are very few Streams of Consciousness created, yet they are welcomed expressions and pathways for direct Divine connection. Each realm fine-tuned their Stream of Consciousness to their own delight. The stream would then resonate to the preferred vibratory pattern and all was good. Every stream was created of the highest spiritual vibration and Divine resonance. All tunings resonated to the highest Divine resonance. Each delighted in the beauty and profound nature of their stream. Sometimes other beings would visit another world's stream just to experience that pattern. Naturally, this was done with expressed permission. A great sharing of wonder and experience is always present in the All. This is so with the streams of energy that are used to awaken a connection to the Divine.

The Mysteries of the Streams of Consciousness

Now, I introduce you to the mysteries of the twelve Streams of Consciousness that are connected to your world and how and why they were created and developed.

The Masters of the Streams are always present to the Singular Outpouring of the Divine. They noticed that the Great Beings found a rich Divine experience through the Original Streams of Consciousness. The Masters of the Streams created the twelve Streams of Consciousness that are the energetic trails that touch the earth as a gift for humanity's guidance. They resonate to and provide a direct, clear, vibrationally sound pathway to the Divine. They were created to be optimal codings and pathways to awaken Divine communion. These streams are humanity's pathways and they are humanity driven.

The Streams of Consciousness that are active on Earth were created to form direct pathways for connecting humanity with the Divine. The twelve Streams of Consciousness, created for humanity, provide focused experiences and awakenings to the Divine. In this way, humanity could and can receive Divine revelation, wisdom and connection through a localized focus and experience unification with the Divine. The Singular Outpouring is vast, infinite and ever-expanding. The Masters of the Streams noticed that it was sometimes more challenging and overwhelming for humanity to find direct experience and illumination from the Singular Outpouring. They created the Streams of Consciousness as a gift for humanity to find a clear, focused conduit and experience of the Divine.

The twelve Streams of Consciousness came to Earth together and have been re-coded and aligned at different times to synchronize with human unfolding. While the twelve Streams of Consciousness relate to the earth body and She does hold them, they are genuinely of little spiritual consequence to the Earth, Herself. The streams are not pathways for the planet, Gaia Terra. She is in Her aligned wholeness.

In their original creation, each of the twelve Streams of Consciousness was available and engaged at different times. All were generally present whether in specific activation or potential activation. Each stream had a small collective of overseers, the Guardians of the Streams, who could and would monitor and adapt the streams to keep them open and in harmony with the theme of the stream and the focus of humanity. Each and every stream is always aligned with the highest Divine frequencies and connection.

There are twelve Streams of Consciousness in all. The number twelve is most sacred on earth. The original intention or purpose or idea, was that a person could select a stream which was in most harmony with how they enjoyed experiencing their Divine connection. They would then resonate with that stream. In this resonance, they would awaken to their connection and be inspired, embraced and illuminated. Each Stream of Consciousness corresponds to a pathway of Divine inspiration. Through any or each or all of these streams an individual or a group can find passage to the Divine. Passage means that energetically an individual could travel within the stream, become attuned to the energies and release the limitations and restrictions of socialized and genetic programming to reach a deep and personal relationship with the Divine All and their own divinity. All streams connect to the Divine at their point of origination. Each stream favors a particular experience of quality which is in harmony with the person who chooses that stream.

The Streams of Consciousness are always connected to the Divine Oneness, the Singular Outpouring. They are never separated. The Streams of Consciousness exist within and vibrate to create trails of specific energy that lead to an individual experience of the Divine. Each stream is aligned with a quality and a system of experiencing Divinity and connection. The twelve Streams of Consciousness on Earth have different tunings and themes of experience to bring a richness of perception and awareness to Divine communion. The focus and delight of the Great Beings, and their own individual experience, inspired them to create the Streams of Consciousness as gifts for humanity. Through their creation of the streams each and every being could dip into the trails of focused energy.

This is the gift of those Great Beings and this is the gift of the Streams of Consciousness for humanity. Through participation with Streams of Consciousness, each individual can infuse themselves with a condensed and convergent energy of Goddess essence knowing all streams lead to the Cosmic All, The Divine One, to the Goddess. We, Alawashka, Lumari and the Masters of Streams of Consciousness, reveal this to you.

CHAPTER TWO:

Within the Streams

All Streams of Consciousness proceed from the center of the Universal All to this planet. When understood and engaged in its true format, any Stream of Consciousness brings true inspiration, illumination and enlightenment and is an unmistakable path to higher spirituality and awakening. Within the Streams of Consciousness, you are invited to experience, resonate to and celebrate the special frequencies that lead to the Divine connection, awakening and expression.

Each Stream of Consciousness is unique and beautiful. Each stream revels in the Divine and celebrates this spiritual communion. The qualities inherent in each stream, bring a special focus to life and awareness. Every individual who experiences this special focus receives inspiration, awakening and spiritual relatedness. Through the individual attuned focus of a stream, a rich appreciation and deep knowing of the Divine becomes present.

The Streams of Consciousness for humanity are direct vibrational paths of experience that lead to the Divine in a specific way. Each stream is a particular tuning. Each stream is aligned with a prominent quality which engages other qualities. Through clear connection to a Stream of

Consciousness, you have a direct route to the Divine through that particular stream's focus. The stream itself attunes you to its prominent quality and the energy patterns of that quality, so you can experience the Divine in a guided and direct manner. The stream aligns you to the essence and qualities it imbues. It can be the most direct route to the Divine. It helps you experience more and more of Divine connection.

Each of humanity's Streams of Consciousness was created by the Masters of the Streams of Consciousness in collaboration with Alawashka's Creation Source Frequencies. The streams are formed in an indescribable way, based on millions of calculations holding the essence of unity in the Singular Outpouring of the Divine, under the direction of the Masters of the Streams. The streams are individually aligned and cognizant. They recognize, understand and work with each individual in a specific, unique relatedness. The Streams of Consciousness are not a fixed system of energy that creates a mass affect which is unrelated to the individual receiving the stream. Each Stream of Consciousness is aware of and in communion with the total individual. The energies, vibrations, qualities and wisdom flow in a respectful agreement and relationship towards a higher Divine expression.

Each of humanity's Streams of Consciousness is overseen by Guardians of the Streams of Consciousness who help attune and watch over the streams that grace your planet, Gaia Terra, and through Her, help hold specific patterns of Divine light for humanity. These wise beings help to contain the essence of each light stream for humanity, always weaving those individual streams into the complex tapestry of universal harmony. Neither the Masters of the Streams of Consciousness or Guardians of the Streams of Consciousness have a human connection or emissary. They are specifically focused upon the stream to which they are aligned, not on individuals. Their work is all-consuming.

Every Stream of Consciousness is an open pathway to experience the fullness of the Divine, the God, the Goddess, the All Encompassing. We reveal these secrets and we reveal the mysteries of the Streams of Consciousness, so you may knowingly choose to connect with and participate with these pathways to direct experience of the Divine. This becomes your conscious choice, your clear opportunity to freely say 'yes' to this portal of Divine embrace.

The Streams of Consciousness are clear, vibrational, spiritual trails of energy that bring you continual, direct access to the Divine. They are created for humanity to open your view and present an invitation to experiences of Divine knowing, presence and illumination in more focused vibrational pathways.

There are twelve Streams of Consciousness created for humanity. Every Stream of Consciousness is an open trail to experience the fullness of the Divine, the God, the Goddess, the All Encompassing, the Divine and the Cosmic All. Each Stream of Consciousness is its own attunement, own focus and vibrational pathway. All Streams of Consciousness can bring you to advanced levels of spiritual awakening, perception and relatedness.

In participation with each Stream of Consciousness, you can expand and grow into the quality or essence of that individual stream. This is a considerable leap of consciousness which benefits the individual and the whole of humanity. It also benefits all life on this planet and in relationship to all life and consciousness everywhere. As one being, one life, expands its knowing and appreciation of the All, then all of life is expanded.

The Streams of Consciousness are always connected to the Divine Oneness, the Singular Outpouring. They are never separated. They exist within this outpouring and vibrate to create trails of specific energy that lead to an individual experience of the Divine.

The Twelve Streams of Consciousness are:
The Stream of Purity
The Stream of Honor
The Stream of Compassion
The Stream of Neutrality
The Stream of Harmony
The Stream of Beauty and Grace
The Stream of Wisdom
The Stream of Truth
The Stream of Radiance
The Stream of Reciprocity
The Stream of Universality
The Stream of Unity

The elegant beauty of each Stream of Consciousness is in its abundant flow and particular vibrational patterns. While the attunement to a flow is personal, the flow itself is Divine. The beauty and capacity of these streams can align you and show you how the resonance can bring the stream and wisdom even closer to their original intent. There is no 'one and only' path to the Divine.

Each person has an opening and resonance and attunements to all Streams of Consciousness. Each person embodies the capacities of each thematic expression of the Divine. The thematic expressions of the Divine that are the specific qualities and tunings of each stream are fully created and compatible with you as a human and Divine being. Those who freely choose to connect with and experience a particular Stream of Consciousness are often more aligned with that stream, more curious about that stream or may appear to have greater tunings to that stream's focus.

Each Stream of Consciousness has its own particular energies that it imparts when an individual or group enters the vibrational patterns of its energies and resonates to those qualities. Each stream is open for a personal connection. It is a matter of whether an individual feels compatible to those energies and is interested in achieving a resonance with that stream. We are revealing the Streams of Consciousness at this time, so you may achieve a resonant relationship with a specific stream and/or all streams, if you so choose. They are no longer hidden from you. Now you may choose these blessed direct pathways to Divine experience and expression.

The Streams of Consciousness are not specifically exclusionary. They are a direct pathway to Divine connection. That is why they were and are created. You may encounter, travel within or commune with any stream. If you feel drawn to a particular stream, you can move into alignment with it and luxuriate in those complex, rich vibrations that lead to direct Divine connection. You may choose to experience another stream at a later time. You may also choose to stay in the frequencies and pathway of one Stream of Consciousness that inspires you and feels in alignment. Celebrate your choices, your experiences of the Divine and the Streams of Consciousness. Each choice, each encounter is a blessing.

You will be able to experience a connection with every Stream of Consciousness, because we are introducing you to each stream in our written description. We reveal the hidden existence of the Streams of Consciousness and introduce you to their resonances, so you have clear access. We reveal the vibrational pathways of each Stream of Consciousness, so you may encounter their resonance in a sacred and clear way, through the words and energies encoded in this book. You will experience your own personal connection in your own way. You may relish the energy of one Stream of Consciousness more than another and you may find a rich harmony with all. Your choice is blessed.

It is true that if every person on this planet moved into resonance with a specific stream, any specific stream, that the harmony and awakening of humanity would be revealed. It is true that one encounter with any of the streams can bring you to a higher, more joyous and appreciative way of life. It is true that experiencing a Stream of Consciousness can open the core of all humanity to an unbridled recognition and appreciation of all life.

Each Stream of Consciousness brings an awareness of the Divine in its own context, and when one chooses to experience a specific individual stream the blessings of that resonance are present. Each Stream has gifts to impart. To move in harmony with this recognition is to understand, respect and appreciate that each may choose their own Divine connection.

When we speak of the Streams of Consciousness and access to them, we speak specifically to those who wish to experience more of the clear Divine energies in their life. Accessing the Streams of Consciousness is not the only and singular way of connecting with and resonating to the higher frequencies of Divine essence. There are many ways of awakening to a greater self-knowing.

Every experience of life leads to the Divine. Awakening to that fact is a powerful understanding. The Divine is within all things, all people, all experiences. This spiritual expansion and communion can unfold within a stream or within the Singular Outpouring of the Divine One. Selecting a stream to participate within can be an expedient way for a spiritual journey.

▲ You can choose to experience a stream, and then later decide to leave that stream.
▲ You can choose to select another stream or travel within the overall flows of spirit.
▲ You can choose to experience a stream and then choose to experience the Singular Outpouring.
▲ You can choose to experience a stream, and then find the guidance in the Divine that is best for you.

Personal knowing will suggest which is most compatible with your inner core, your soul's calling, your personal resonating frequencies, your own beliefs, your social relationships, your community and your environment.

If you do not want to experience the Streams of Consciousness, that is a choice that is appropriate to you. It is also true that this may not be your individual path or choice. You may also choose to explore and travel in spiritual connections that are not held in the Streams of Consciousness and are a different focus of vibration and experience. All choices are honored in the great journey of awakening to the Divine All and One.

Many people throughout time have aligned with, entered and participated with Streams of Consciousness, knowingly or not. Many individuals felt their Divine connection and lived in a state of gracious harmony with their path and their earthly life. They received Divine inspiration, helped their communities and families, learned new ways of adapting, discovered new methods for civilization and contributed greatly to human life on this planet. They communed with the Streams of Consciousness and their individual lives benefited all life on this planet. This has been so since the beginning and it flows today.

We reveal the existence of the Streams of Consciousness, because these pathways and highways have been hidden, and therefore even if you traveled within one of the Streams of Consciousness, you did not specifically know that you had chosen that avenue of spiritual expression. Many people resonated with Streams of Consciousness, and yet had no knowledge or understanding of their participation.

Today that is different.

We reveal the frequencies of the Streams of
Consciousness and you are invited to explore.
In honor of your wholeness and beauty,
we invite you.

CHAPTER THREE:

Revelations and Requests

We are revealing the existence of the Streams of Consciousness for many reasons. Now is the time for many changes on Earth and many opportunities for change. There are new energies, new frequencies coming into focus that can help awaken a greater connection to the Divine for all people and beings. We are disclosing the wisdom of the streams, so you can understand the long journey humanity has taken in resonance with the Divine. The Streams of Consciousness have remained hidden knowledge.

Another reason for revealing the long held secrets of the Streams of Consciousness is so you can access the beauty of any stream and travel into the Divine wholeness from that unique perspective. You may feel more in harmony with one focus or another. Each stream is a magnificent attunement of Divine light, held in a unique resonant perspective. We have attuned the words of this book to the energy of the Streams of Consciousness. You will have straight access to experiencing the streams. Therefore, this will help you to bypass any codified training of the past and feel the clear energies present within the stream.

These revelations will also help you understand the inner life of people from different cultures and even different times. The Earth is rich with diversity. This book reveals that the Streams of Consciousness exist. The revelations in this book and the descriptions of each stream provide you with a new perceptive in relating to all of the cultures of this planet. As you receive greater understanding as to the nature of the spiritual influences touching humanity and can feel and experience the streams that have helped shape spiritual relatedness, you can increase your compassion and relatedness to all people and beings. This will help awaken the deeper dreams of humanity. It will help bring about the global awakening and deep community that is the vision and dream of this time.

Human nature is curious. Humanity loves to explore. It is important to follow a path of exploration if it calls to you. It is also important to honor that very path and the landscape of it. Each person is always responsible for their own actions and the effects of those actions in the universe. Before Lumari began to write this book, which reveals the existence of the Streams of Consciousness and reveals some deeper revelations about teachers, masters and humanity, we asked for express permission to reveal this information to humanity at this time. We do not reveal it, simply because we have the information and know it. This would be a breach of honor and integrity. Just because something exists and is known, does not mean it is to be revealed. Doing so would dishonor the energy of the streams, which would then alter your experience of it.

We asked for permission.

We asked for permission from the Masters and Guardians of every stream and every being who has worked with, calibrated, taught, enhanced and directs the energies of the Streams of Consciousness. If any one of them had told us they did not want this to unfold, we would not share the information.

We honor them. We honor their place and their work and their knowing. We received express permission to reveal the nature of the streams with very specific guidelines and agreements as to the way this would be revealed. We listened to their requests and guidance. We also agreed to administer their specific requests to put forward to you. By asking for and receiving express permission to reveal the nature and vibrations of the Streams of Consciousness, we agreed to the requests of the Guardians of the Streams. We also agreed to share their requests with you. As you are now part of this revelation and teaching, the guardians and guides have asked us to request your help in certain areas. We ask you to honor their requests.

The Request Of The Guardians

The Frequencies Of Honor

When revealing hidden vibrations, wisdom and teachings, it is important to be in the space of honoring the reciprocal spiritual space, teachings and beings. This creates a powerful sacred space in which the wisdom is shared, the highest vibrations are held, and the revelations can be received. Before we chose to reveal the Streams of Consciousness, we entered a sacred space of honor. We extended honor to the Divine, to the Masters of the Streams and the Guardians of the Streams who have agreed to share this with you and make it available in this now.

Now, we extended honor to the vibrations and awareness of the Streams of Consciousness. Sharing the Streams of Consciousness is a blessing. As we create a space of honor, we also extend this honor to you, you who are receiving the secret wisdom and teachings of the Streams of Consciousness, and you who will resonate and receive these blessings.

Extending honor is a very advanced practice of being. This one frequency and practice elevates all beings in the Divine. We also ask that, as you read this book, as you feel these energies and teachings, and as you expand your awareness herein, that you first extend honor to yourself. Honor your life and your journey and the pathways that led you to this moment in time. We honor you, dear one.

Please extend honor to the Masters of the Streams and the Guardians of the Streams and honor the majesty of the Streams of Consciousness that will now be revealed to you.

In this honoring, you now enter a sacred space and a frequency of being that is more open to receive these many blessings. This space holds the highest frequencies of honor and grows to invite the highest blessings for you. Thank you.

Now we share the honor and share:
THE REQUEST OF THE GUARDIANS.
In this space of reciprocal honor, The Guardians of the Streams and the beings aligned with them ask that you respect and honor the nature of their undertaking. They ask that you honor and respect this work, this explanation and revelation of the Streams of Consciousness. They ask that you respect the truth of origination, creation and the work that all of us have done to bring the information, teachings and vibrational access of the streams to you.
Please, agree to honor this request. Say 'yes' now.

The Guardians of the Streams and beings working with and aligned with the Streams of Consciousness for Humanity ask that you do not alter any aspect of any stream you encounter. The streams do not need to be altered or changed, no matter what you observe or intuit.

The Streams of Consciousness are attended by and recalibrated in the greatest attention to Humanity and the Divine, by very highly advanced beings. It is best that if you want to learn more about the streams that you flow through them and feel the blessings they impart or that you watch the changes from an interested and respectful distance.
Please, agree to honor this request. Say 'yes' now.

The Guardians of the Streams and the beings aligned with them ask that you do not endeavor to contact them. Please understand that they do not wish to be contacted. They will not answer a request for contact or guidance. They do not want you to assume that aligning with any stream confers to you the truth and guidance of that stream as a chosen one, or guide, or teacher, or designated authority of the stream. This request of non-contact also extends to the Great Beings and Masters of the Streams, mentioned earlier in this book. The blessing of the revelation of the Streams of Consciousness, now, is that you may access them and receive the blessings, awakenings and wisdom.

There are many beings in the Universal All who do not wish to be contacted by others. It is very important to honor and accept that request. Imagine how many people can now become aware of the Streams of Consciousness and the guardians and other guides affiliated with the streams because of this book. The permission from the Guardians enabled us to write this and divulge these unknown and untold teachings and pathways in a very in-depth manner. Each and every person reading this book or hearing about it may want to make contact with a being. They may have questions to ask. They may want guidance. They may want to learn how to alter and shift the streams. The guardians, guides and affiliated beings do not want to and will not answer questions or give guidance and training to anyone. They are not teachers or trainers or conduits of energy. They are the Guides and Guardians of the Streams with vast responsibilities in other concentrations. Allow the inspiration, awakenings and transformations from the Streams of Consciousness to be your own guidance. This is the brilliance of the Streams of Consciousness.

Please, agree to honor this request. Say 'yes' now.

The Guardians of the Stream invite you to participate within the Streams of Consciousness. This book is written is to help you understand how a particular stream holds certain vibrational themes of experience. Through your own participation, through honoring these paths and requests, you have access to pathways of Divine connection that are endless, rich and aligned for you. You will see and understand how to hold an energy and perspective that allows you to honor and appreciate the many gifts of spirit, while traveling on your preferred path.

By understanding the true attunements of each stream, you will have deep understanding of the heart of humanity. You will be able to appreciate all of the subtleties and blessings held in the inner resting places of all people. You will begin to understand the differences between what they strive for in each stream and what they have received. Through this understanding, you will receive the blessings and teachings of each pathway.

Please, agree to honor this request and invitation. Say 'yes.'

Blessings

Blessings to you and your illuminating,
awakening journey
within the Streams of Consciousness.

CHAPTER FOUR:

Personal Participation

The Streams of Consciousness were created to help all of humanity receive the blessings of the Divine through powerful attunements. They are created to open a direct connection that is an access to the Divine in a more focused manner. As Lumari and I reveal the streams to you, you will be able to gently touch the essence of each stream. Each stream is a theme of experience which will open that expression of the Divine within you. Initially, you will experience the flavor of a stream. Later, as you continue to engage with a stream, more and more alignment will unfold. Often, it takes time and it takes practice to flow in harmony with a Stream of Consciousness. Give yourself the gift of time.

All Streams of Consciousness are open and available to you. We give names to the streams, because the names will help you to encounter each stream most easily. Therefore, these names will guide you to the streams most effectively.

All Streams of Consciousness have the same measure of energy. One stream is not more powerful than another. Each has a particular frequency alignment, but all contain the same level of energy and all are connected to the Divine. The names given to the streams are the names that will most attune you to the essence and original frequencies of those streams of energy. They were not originally named anything. The names provided for these streams will help you track the essence of a stream and therefore recognize when you have encountered it. This will guide your alignment and illumination.

In each chapter, we introduce you to one of the twelve Streams of Consciousness. As we mentioned, this book is more than a description of the streams. This book is encoded with entry codes, attunements, advanced vibrations and openings, so you may embark on a knowing journey. This is a direct introduction to the energies, frequencies and teachings of each stream.

How To Approach A Stream

It may be best for your own personal integrity, your human form and spiritual energy, if you gently encounter one stream. This will help you understand the nature of the stream, its inherent pathways and how its energies interact with your own. As you begin to read about each Stream of Consciousness, read that chapter and then pause. Let yourself experience the beauty of that stream. Each stream is very powerful. Contact with any Stream of Consciousness can be a life-altering experience. In honor and respect for your body and your spiritual alignment, touch the stream of your choice very lightly and allow the process of discovery to unfold. Then if you wish to proceed further, your process of awakening and your travels will be more graceful.

The most beneficial way of connecting with a stream is through carrying the qualities of honor, harmony and appreciation. Honor, harmony and appreciation are reciprocal.

To engage the stream of your choice, you must first honor yourself. Understand, honor and respect who you are and whether this stream or focus is appropriate for you at this time.

If this is so, and you wish to engage with the stream, then you extend that respect to the energies and Guardians of the Stream itself.

Honoring yourself and honoring the stream, creates an opening of harmony. You become harmonious with the stream.

Through the honor and harmony, this creates the appropriate resonance of appreciation, so you may experience your own being, the wisdom and attunements of the stream and receive greater knowing.

When the qualities of honor, harmony and appreciation are present in your approach and participation, you will be in alignment in a more gracious way.

It is still possible to connect with a stream while having a certain amount of confusion in this area, but it can be more challenging. In the highest regard for your essence and being and path of growth, hold the focus of harmony within. Harmony can hold many notes - all in perfect accord. Each stream and pathway is in perfect harmony with Divine resonance. Each stream is in direct connection to the Divine. As you learn to hold the qualities of honor, harmony and appreciation within you, you will gain greater and more profound access to the Streams of Consciousness and to all Divine aspects of the Great All and One. As we explore deeper into the themes and Divine energies of each Stream of Consciousness, you will begin to notice what each stream can provide.

Approach the stream with awareness. You will notice an alteration in your personal vibration upon encountering any stream. Perceptions may be keener, emotions smoother and an atmosphere of connection and blessing will be evident. You may also feel exhilaration, transformation and illumination. Allow yourself to become comfortable with the essence and energy of the stream. Pay attention to your being. Do not allow yourself to become overzealous or too eager. Be patient in your connection and be open to receiving. There is no work to do here. You do not need to try anything or do anything specific. You enter a stream to partake of its splendor, qualities and its specific pathways of connection to the Divine All. The vast capacities and blessings within any stream can be overwhelming, so allow yourself the grace and ease of your own exploration.

Approach any and every stream with dignity. Encountering a stream is like beginning a new relationship. Be easy and be within yourself. Be earnest in your approach and considerate in your connection, just as you would in beginning a relationship with someone you care for deeply. Do not go stream-hopping. As you read this book, you will be introduced to every stream and you will have a clear personal experience of its energies. We have chosen the order and sequence of the streams to align with the utmost blessings. Later, you can go back to connect with and read again about the specific Stream of Consciousness that calls to you. Allow yourself the time to learn and experience. Allow the stream time to reveal itself to you. While you may experience the gifts of a stream the moment you engage, it can also take many months of connection to begin to understand the qualities and nature of any stream. Many individuals have chosen to resonate with one stream for their whole life and delight in the brilliance and their personal gifts and alignment. Each stream is a multi-dimensional experience and can never be fully known. Yet, with time, connection and openness, you will reap blessings beyond your present understanding.

Resonating with a Stream of Consciousness

When an individual is resonating within the energies of a specific stream, they will have a clearer understanding of the qualities activated by that stream. When you are resonating with a stream, you experience the qualities, knowing and wisdom the stream imparts. You may see the world through that clear resonance. You may also experience and know a deep interconnectedness through the focus of that special stream. Your resonance and alignment are an ongoing experience and grows with time. All Streams of Consciousness resonate with a collective focus and through that resonance create a direct connection with the Divine.

Most people encounter a stream and resonate with it. This is a symbiotic, collaborative participation. You may flow with the energies, feel the wisdom, vibrate in attunement and experience the gifts, understanding and blessed perceptions that lead to direct Divine connection in a clear, gracious and uplifting way.

An individual who is resonating within the Stream of Compassion, will feel compassion for others and for your world. You will be moved and motivated by a deep feeling of alignment and kindness toward humanity, animals and the planet, Herself. You will also feel that life and people will benefit from more compassion. You will act more compassionately and those actions, which could reveal themselves in so many different ways, will be guided by a caring, supportive and tender way of relating to the world.

As we describe the twelve individual Streams of Consciousness in the upcoming chapters, our focus is on an individual who is resonating with a particular stream. We reveal the energies in play and the transformations that generate sacred relatedness.

Influenced by a Stream of Consciousness

When an individual is influenced by a person or a community that is attuned to the qualities of a Stream of Consciousness, then you will appreciate the qualities and wisdom of that stream.

You will appreciate the power and wisdom of that stream's gifts. You are not attuned to them and may not be resonating with them. You simply recognize, respect and appreciate them. An individual who is influenced by a community resonating with the Stream of Wisdom, will appreciate the ancient knowing and the stories that evoke a respect and alliance with wisdom in its highest sense. All Streams of Consciousness have been resonating on this planet since ancient times and have influenced the individual lives and the many communities of humanity. The individual influenced by a particular stream will recognize and appreciate those elegant qualities, while you may be resonating to another Stream of Consciousness or flowing in the Singular Outpouring. You may be surprised at how you are influenced by many different Streams of Consciousness in your life.

Illuminated by a Stream of Consciousness

An individual can also be illuminated by a Stream of Consciousness. Illumination brings a greater level of attunement to the energies of the stream. The individual being illuminated will begin to alter their personal resonance in harmony with the specific Stream of Consciousness that they have encountered. This is a very special and often dramatic event. The first touch of a stream, the first energies of illumination are life-altering and profound. Connecting with a Stream of Consciousness in this fashion creates immediate shifts and changes in perception. You feel an opening to the deeper meanings and mysteries of life. The experience is concentrated. Truths of perception and greater wisdom are shared and sometimes revealed. The most distinct aspect of an illuminating connection with a Stream of Consciousness is that the individual feels as though their questions have been answered and that they know, unequivocally, that they have been touched by or connected with a source of Divine presence.

Does this feel familiar to you? Have you experienced an illuminating, connection of insight, knowing, clarity and transformation that changed your life? Have you felt as though you were touched by the Divine? Have you awakened to a greater knowing, and been blessed with an awareness that goes beyond your normal understanding? Have you felt quickened by the enlightening brilliance that shifted your life in beautiful ways? Have you had life-changing experiences that feel Divinely inspired and have moved you to a new way of knowing and being? Have you felt a spiritual awakening, a direct contact with the Divine that has vibrationally shifted your soul and being? If you have experienced any of these, it is likely you have been illuminated by a Stream of Consciousness.

Each stream has touched the deep spiritual core of people who have risen beyond their own knowing to shape a new vision and a new life for humanity. When individuals and groups of people are moved to create a higher vision of their world, when they exceed the known confines of their community, when they awaken to a larger view and a new possibility for life, then it is most likely they have been illuminated by a Stream of Consciousness. Those people who have been illuminated perceive this change as a blessing and sometimes a calling.

People who have all been illuminated by a Stream of Consciousness have felt a new and profound connection to their personal calling. Each person, when aligned with that stream and moving within that new attunement, has changed the perceptions of the world. They have been inspired and have provided the inspiration for others to proceed with them, and then move forward in that resonance. Most people are either resonating with or influenced by a Stream of Consciousness. They contribute to the world by their lives and help fulfill the evolution of this world and this planet by their participation with their chosen stream.

Those people who are illuminated by a Stream of Consciousness have much more energy from that stream. Therefore, they are more greatly filled with the attunements of their experience and the specific qualities of that stream. By the illumination of the stream, their lives and perceptions are altered. They hold specific frequencies that resonate with the stream of choice and they usually alter their lives accordingly. The new realizations that occur bring these individuals the energy, impetus and designs that change their lives and the lives of those they encounter. Sometimes these are the people who quit their jobs, sell all of their possessions and start anew. Sometimes these are the people who seize something new and different and dedicate their lives to its creation. And while not all people who are illuminated by the Stream of Consciousness go out and radically change the world, each person does go through a profound, dramatic and significant change that alters the course of their lives. Does this sound or feel familiar to you?

Experiencing a Stream of Consciousness

Many people are touched by the energies of a particular Stream of Consciousness and are moved beyond their usual perceptions. A new awareness occurs when the stream and the individual meet in resonance. Their energies connect and the first touch of the Stream of Consciousness caresses the individual participant. For most individuals, this is more than enough. Being touched by the resonance of a stream is an unforgettable experience. For many, this is the moment that they have an epiphany. They gain a rare clarity and view of how all life works. They feel touched by the presence of Spirit, directly, in that moment. They know that in this very instant of time, they have had a powerful spiritual experience and that they have touched the Divine in some way. This experience of spiritual revelation is a reciprocal event. The energies of the Stream of Consciousness, in connection with the Divine, the Goddess, have made a graceful contact with this particular person. The person's energies have shifted to embrace and recognize the specific qualities within that stream.

An individual will only come into contact with a Stream of Consciousness that is compatible with them and their personal path or destiny. In this way, the individual is more graciously transformed and uplifted. The individual begins to resonate with the stream and the qualities inherent within the stream, while simultaneously forming a sacred bridge with the Divine. Their inner being uses the stream as it is intended to be used. Their inner being uses the stream as a conduit, through which they can easily and gracefully connect with the Divine as an outer expression and also connect with the Divine as an inner expression. The outer expression of the Divine is the knowing and presencing of the true and sacred forces of the universe in all locations and times. The inner expression of the Divine is the knowing and presencing of the true and sacred forces within one's own being. They resonate together and blossom as one garden. The Stream of Consciousness provides the pathway and vibrational container for this experience.

Through connecting with and experiencing the energies of a Stream of Consciousness, you will also be able to heal judgments and preconceived notions that have distorted the interpretations of the true essence of the stream within yourself and within humanity as a whole. This healing takes place through personal understanding. It is not a doing. There is nothing to do in a stream. It is a perceptive experience of being.

Therefore, if you move into resonance with an aspect of a stream and notice releases of energy, emotion or an alteration of a perspective or belief that has limited you, this is a healing. This is a blessing. As each person reads about the Streams of Consciousness and becomes familiar with the qualities of the streams, preconceived notions and restrictions can melt away. Through this new resonance and appreciation, each person can release energy that has been counterproductive for their personal life. Each person can also release energy, judgments and prejudices that are restrictive in the whole of earth's population.

By understanding and appreciating the true energies and qualities of the Streams of Consciousness, each individual can release and heal the misconceptions and misinterpretations within themselves. This release and reorientation can affect not only the present life you are living, but it can also reach back into time to release and heal past life issues and confusions that may affect this lifetime. Still continuing with this level of healing and restoration, as the energies of past life hurts and misconceptions are healed and repaired through connection with the appropriate resonance of the Streams of Consciousness, then other people who were affected by an individual's actions will also have the opportunity to heal those hurts in their past lives as well. This suggests that in your own shift into greater awareness and healing, you provide the opportunity for others to heal as well, simply by your own emancipation. This does indeed create a powerful healing for the person and very directly, for the world. This is a possible and likely aspect of working with a Stream of Consciousness and becoming oriented to the qualities of the Divine within it.

Within a Stream of Consciousness

Once traveling within a Stream of Consciousness, let the honor, harmony and appreciation flow in a reciprocal loop through you, into the stream and back to you. Be in harmony with your own being and energy. You do not have to be overzealous in your exuberance for the blessings of the stream. Allow the blessings to unfold gracefully within yourself. Know when you have had enough, and respect yourself for that knowing. Be open to the communion of the stream. If you feel there is more for you to experience at this time, then honor your being and ask if this is true. If you want that deep experience, gift that to yourself. If this is so, be graceful and gracious with your being. There is no need to overload your energy. If you feel you want to take it slower, then honor your knowing.

In this regard, if the stream begins to disengage from you, you are done. Respect that and release the energies of the stream. If the stream does not wish to be encountered, honor that position. You must honor your own being. If there appears to be more available and yet your body is tired, let it go. Honor the totality of your being. Honor the totality of the streams and the guardians. Then, in time and in blessings, you will know the true heart of humanity and be able to nourish and uplift the lives of all.

The Streams of Consciousness were initially created to help all of humanity receive the blessings of the Divine through powerful attunements. They are created to open a direct connection that is an access to the Divine in a more focused manner.

Follow your heart and your inner guidance to explore each stream and celebrate the Divine.

As you read each chapter about each Stream of Consciousness, you are being introduced to that stream, its vibrations, alignment and pathway. You will gain an understanding and an opportunity for direct Divine connection.

As you read about and encounter each Stream of Consciousness, you may find some of them are familiar to you. You may feel a deeper connection and understanding that you 'know this' or 'remember this.' When this is so, then you have indeed previously encountered this specific Stream of Consciousness. You may have unknowingly met this energy in this lifetime. This may be the Stream of Consciousness that calls you forward into being. It may be the stream that is at the heart of your soul and perspective in this life. The Streams of Consciousness have inspired and influenced many individuals, many groups, many cultures and societies on this planet.

You may also feel a longing for this stream. It may feel like you have been waiting for this stream all of your life. If you feel the connection, if your heart opens and soars and your soul feels the gratitude, you may have flowed with this Stream of Consciousness in a past or concurrent lifetime.

Smile! Welcome back!

Flowing In This Book

When you are reading about an individual Stream of Consciousness, you are being introduced to that stream, its vibrations and wisdom. You have an opportunity for direct Divine connection. Here are some suggestions as possible ways to read and connect with the revealed mysteries of the streams, so you may be centered, present and even more blessed.

You may read about each Stream of Consciousness from the beginning and in the sequential order in which the streams are presented. This sequence helps you experience each Stream of Consciousness in an aligned and awakening flow. This is how our book and journey are designed.

You may want to read all the way through the whole book, first. Then, you may choose to circle back to select the Stream of Consciousness that calls to you at that time. You may continue to read that chapter many times and experience resonating with and growing with that specific Stream of Consciousness.

You may choose one Stream of Consciousness that calls to you or feels aligned with you. You may want to read about that one Stream of Consciousness several times, allowing the energy, alignment and blessing to grow. You may choose one Stream of Consciousness chapter that you read every day as a practice and blessing. The energies and Divine connection will continue to expand. You may want to engage with that Stream of Consciousness for a time.

You may want to read the whole book from beginning to end in one collective experience. Sometimes your inner alignment and exuberance wants to expand in a saturated, immersed way to experience it all. If this is you, do check your energies and honor your being. Read in sacred saturation.

You may want to take your time and become personally saturated within each stream. You may want to experience the nuances and wisdom therein. If this is you, do check your energies and honor your being.

You may feel that while you are reading the streams in sequence, that you are not ready for a particular Stream of Consciousness. You may feel you would like to skip reading about and encountering that stream for the moment. This is your wisdom to follow. Skip that stream and select another.

Each time you read any chapter in this book, whether it is about the individual Streams of Consciousness or the wisdom held herein, you will receive the frequencies of highest blessings. This book is encoded and calibrated to bring blessings that are in alignment with you.

When you are more familiar with each stream, you may wish to explore a stronger connection to one particular stream over time. Time reveals many mysteries.

As you read about each Stream of Consciousness, we are introducing you to that stream. Every chapter is an introduction and an encounter. As you read about each stream, you are making a connection with that stream. The words in this book are created, infused and activated to help you and open you to that awareness, if you wish. You may experience a beautiful resonance, understanding, shift and transformation by reading the chapter for each Stream of Consciousness. You may experience a feeling of knowing, a heart-warming, understanding and shift into deeper wisdom and joy. We are creating a direct contact and attunement to each Stream of Consciousness by describing it in certain ways and holding its vibrational frequency within the text herein. This is experiential. You will be introduced, thereby making a graceful and compatible connection, making it easier for you to connect with and distinguish each Stream of Consciousness. Then, when you read and engage in Calling Forth the Streams of Consciousness, you will be in greater knowing to experience attunement with each Stream of Consciousness in a much more profound and enlightening way.

When you begin to recognize the underlying focus of a stream and its remarkable vibrational pathways that lead to Divine encounter, you will be able to see how the energies work and unfold. You will be able to feel the more pristine aspects of these Divine blessings. You will begin to distinguish the rich subtleties of each stream and its exquisite energies and profound truths. Each Stream of Consciousness will reveal, enlighten and gift you with a unique and direct pathway to the Divine. Use your own soul, your own resonance and your own experience to explore and open to these sacred and now revealed gifts.

Now, you are ready to discover the wisdom and frequencies of each individual Stream of Consciousness.

As a reminder, to gain a deeper experience and understanding of the Streams Of Consciousness, download your free Activations Journal and get more free gifts at www.CosmicStreams.com

Blessings

May you feel and know the gifts of these revelations.
May sacred wisdom, appreciation
and blessings light your way!

PART 2

Initiation

The Twelve Streams of Consciousness

CHAPTER FIVE:

The Stream of Purity

clear embrace of Divine essence
awakens the splendors
light shatters illusions in a spectacle of miracles
to reveal the pristine wonders present in being

The Stream of Purity

The Stream of Purity is an infusion of Divine blessing, light
and frequency that allows and encourages a direct experience
of the Divine, and still helps maintain personal knowing and
integration. This stream creates a clear experience of Divine
energies and connection and opens the high vibrations of
Divine clarity, recognition, awe and inspiration.

When a person enters and resonates with the Stream of Purity,
the brilliance of the Divine and the brilliance of this Divine
connection and revelation, becomes whole. The Stream of
Purity brings an immediate experience of awakening and
revelation. It may be described as Enlightenment. Those who
have experienced the Stream of Purity are illuminated. They
perceive more of their Divine nature, Divine connection and
the resonance of the All.

The Invitation of the Stream of Purity

The Stream of Purity activates and aligns individual, personal experience into a clear and present connection to the Divine. It reorients an individual toward a direct experience of the Divine by eliminating or recalibrating inconsistencies in the vibratory patterns. The stream extends a systematic acceleration of all energy patterns and awakens a uniting flow. It is distinctly powerful and immediate. Through the overlaying patterns of the Stream of Purity and the resonating patterns of the individual, a channel is awakened that bridges the personal and the Divine in one moment.

Contact with the Stream of Purity is contact with pure Divine light. It enters the individual and washes those personal energies that have become discordant or weak or misaligned. The individual is infused with Divine light. All aspects that do not resonate with the higher vibratory patterns and frequencies of the Divine are accelerated, reoriented or cleansed. The individual becomes illuminated by the stream and radiates with this powerful anointing quality of alignment with and attunement to the Divine in all aspects of life and being.

Personal experience of the Stream of Purity is profound and intense. It is a reorientation. The cells of the body vibrate with a clear light. The initial emotional state can be described as awe. Every aspect of being is simultaneously awakened and connected to Divine essence.

The Stream of Purity illuminates energies to bring a focus of the Divine to those people who can move into harmony with the stream and travel within it. By entering the Stream of Purity, the resonance of the energy field is altered to release and reorient the person and all systems toward direct experience of the Divine.

Looking at purity in its sense of vibratory frequency, purity is the recalibration of the human essence into a pattern that is more in harmony with Divine energy, experience and source.

Purity is truly what happens when you resonate with the frequencies of the Divine and receive the energies of that communion. In this you are able to hold more light, more Divine radiance. You are able to release the patterns or beliefs which inhibit that experience. You are able to change ways of being or respond to life in ways that enhance your life, community and the expression of Divine flow. Purity brings light into the areas of being to retune them into higher forms of Divine communion and expression.

Purity is a constant. All beings look toward the energies of purity to feel and receive new awakening into divinity. No matter how experienced, ascended or illuminated a being is, the Divine is always a completely vast and unknowable essence which is in constant awakening and expansion of being. Therefore, no matter how much you know, or how advanced you are, you are always in the presence of more. To experience growth and awakening, the systems and recalibrations of purity are one way of receiving those attunements within your own being. The Stream of Purity baths you in light and helps retune or illuminate the systems of energy or patterns of being which may limit your experience of your Divine connection.

Encountering the Stream of Purity can create a gentle combustion. Energy fields can alter, and even your intellect can reformulate previous teachings and understandings. You may encounter the Divine Oneness of all being and become changed. This encounter is purifying. It releases and clears some of the cloudiness of personal perceptions and brings a deeper understanding of your relationship with the One and the All. Through this experience your whole life is illuminated and changed.

The Invocation of the Stream of Purity

The Stream of Purity releases, reorganizes and illuminates every aspect of being to a clear and pure resonance, so that one can experience the Divine without the clouded perceptions that life may heap upon an individual. It works with every aspect of being. If there are beliefs that thwart or hinder or block Divine recognition, these are illuminated and released. If there are emotional considerations that need to be cleared or repatterned, then these are changed. If there are energy blocks or pathways that are not aligned in concert with the Divine essence for a direct experience of the Divine, then these too, are changed, reorganized and realigned to the highest experience of spiritual communion for each individual.

This illumination may happen in one encounter and the individual will feel an awakening and change in being and perceptions and understanding. This illumination and transformation will happen over time as the individual continues to connect with and embrace the frequencies and awakenings of this stream. The Stream of Purity is a more solitary stream. Solitary meaning that the process of purity is a solo experience. The purity patterns and energies reorganize one's entire system. Each level of discord is altered. Each area of separation from the Divine is changed to resonate with clarity.

This particular stream can be the most demanding of streams to enter and with which to resonate. It can also be the most blissful and exhilarating. It holds a very highly refined light pattern which can be experienced as illumination or as combustion. It illuminates the patterns or systems that hamper resonance with the Divine. In this light, the patterns, beliefs and blocks combust and burn away. Then the stream reorients all of the patterns or missing pieces, as it were, and realigns them to access the Divine.

Upon entering the stream, one is flooded with light. This light, which is specifically attuned to its own process, bathes the individual engaging with the stream. The vibrational sequences of the light and the attunement of the stream reverberate through the individual and retune and recalibrate their every pattern and energy system. Understanding this, entering or receiving the energy of the Stream of Purity is a transformational experience in its truest sense. Patterns, fields, beliefs, assumptions, limitations and ways of experiencing life are transformed - their forms are specifically altered. The term transformation is generally used as a catch-all word. Here, transformation is a very specific alteration in life force and in life perception. Transformation is a permanent change toward greater and more expanded experience. The Stream of Purity brings specific light and vibrational systems into the individual which create a permanent alteration and augmentation toward Divine communion, perception and relatedness. The Stream of Purity purifies the individual of all aspects of being which could hinder Divine communion and knowing. This alters and transforms an individual toward greater receptivity to the Divine, greater alignment with higher spiritual energies and enhanced perception of all life as an endless reverberation of the One and the All.

The Experience of the Stream of Purity

Primary encounters of entering and experiencing the Stream of Purity are life altering. Life does not look like it did before entering and being realigned with this stream. The intensity of the experience of transformation on the personal level does bring about a disorientation and reorientation.

On the emotional level, reasons and motivations for particular actions or ways of being can completely shift. An individual's personal perspective and motivation toward life will naturally shift when the reasons for why he does what he does have been eliminated or realigned with a greater truth and a vaster perspective. On the intellectual level, altered perceptions and different motivations require a reorganization of the intellect, the ways one translates experience into a cognizant form.

Spiritually, the Stream of Purity reorganizes and realigns all aspects of being, perceiving and knowing, by way of altering and enhancing the vibratory patterns that make up the energy bodies and infuses this through and beyond the cellular levels. For someone unaccustomed to this energy or to the process of transformation, this can feel like an all-consuming fire burning through their entire being. At times, this can be felt even with an initial contact with the stream. Becoming aligned with and working within the blessings and gifts of any stream becomes an ongoing path to enlightenment and Divine connection. Each encounter and participation with the stream augments and aligns an individual to this experience. The Stream of Purity, working with and holding the energies, patterns and vibrational frequencies of purity, will continually realign, infuse and release the aspects of a person which are counterproductive to the experience of connectedness to spirit. Each encounter with the Stream of Purity will continue to enhance the complete recalibration process.

The Stream of Purity is transformational. It alters the whole being down to and beyond the cellular levels. The closer you are in alignment to the stream, the more transformation takes place. This transformation alters and augments the emotional, mental and spiritual bodies. It purifies them of contradictions and attunes them to the Divine through a purity process. It also reorganizes the biology of each individual to be able to receive and work with this particular frequency. The cellular structure is changed to hold these patterns and to move toward a more refined spiritual communion and union.

The Stream of Purity and the energies of transformation available through this stream do have the most immediate effect on one's energy fields. This stream can be more intense and concentrated than any other stream. In a certain respect it can be more intense, as generally people would rather feel something as opposed to release something and then retune it. The Stream of Purity releases, reorganizes, recalibrates and transforms every aspect of being that can limit Divine connection and relatedness. It then creates new vibrational patterns that will hold and fine-tune these connections and any new patterns that can and will develop.

Aligning with the Stream of Purity takes time and awareness. It can be viewed as the cornerstone of all other streams. Each aspect and each stream does impart a different relationship or different pathway with the Divine. Purity can be its own path or it can be the resource to connect with the other streams. The Stream of Purity may also be used as a supporting energy to a different Stream of Consciousness. In this manner, one could move in alignment with the Stream of Purity to release and recalibrate one's fields to be more in line with Divine essence. When this unfolds, then one could move into affiliation with another stream to experience that particular resonance and that unique relational tuning with Divine energy.

The Stream of Purity brings continuous connection with Divinity in all aspects, and it will help release and reattune all of your systems to receive and participate with the Divine. It combusts and enlightens the core of being. Through this the clarity of vision, the depths of Divine relatedness shine through every aspect of one's being. This sublime process of connection and renewal brings a powerful and luminous awakening to all aspects of life.

The Influences from the Stream of Purity

The energies, qualities and perspective arising from the Stream of Purity celebrates clarity in all ways of being, thinking and doing. You may want to experience the most aligned energy of any given situation. You want the knowing, the direct experience before others translate it into their own point of view. You may want to enjoy quietude to tune in to the flows of all life and also for specific experiences, so you can reach into that knowing directly. You can see beyond the moment and still celebrate the moment. In many ways you are not attached to your own ideology, except that you favor a clear, transformational experience and knowing. You are very flexible in your being as you know that something new, something expansive and something awakening is a welcome part of your life. You are happy to be your own clear expression of direct experience. You are fluid in your being, while focused in your knowing.

How may the Stream of Purity influence your life?

Personal Vision inspired by the Stream of Purity

You may want to let go of distractions and be in a pure space of knowing more than most people. It's a gift you have to disregard the superfluous and focus on and celebrate the crux, the essence, the clear resonance of Divine energy and of any circumstance. You love to go deep within to see, feel and know from the higher perspective and also from your soul's knowing. You admire and appreciate the clarity, brilliance and quintessence of a system of knowing, a situation and an experience.

You may wonder at the profound essence that many people do not even see, because you can see the clear, pristine brilliance at the center of elaboration. You can feel and know the core that inspires all things to shine and evolve.

Relatedness inspired by the Stream of Purity

Relatedness as inspired by purity, brings a singular connection in its most devoted and respectful way. You see the depths and brilliance of a person's core and you are moved. In your relationships you want to know the depths and create that beautiful connection through knowing truths, depths and what helps an individual shine. You acknowledge the individual beyond the outer presentation, so you can celebrate and appreciate the richness of their soul and their being. You reflect your own authentic self to them and admire their authentic expression and being. In community and groups, you want it real. You want it clear and shining without the embellishments. You see the beauty, wisdom and power in a pure message and the essence of things. For you this is the bottom line, the wholeness without personal interpretation.

You seek a way of purity to bring a clear, direct way to relate, support and bring greater knowing into each person's life. You are a person who listens for the essence in each person and celebrates their own truth, expression and knowing. You shine when pure essence is present, and you reflect that to others in most powerful uplifting ways.

World View inspired by the Stream of Purity

Purity in a world view or cosmic view opens clear paths of appreciation and recognition. You may seek out ways to help people get to a deeper knowing and connection that eliminates the opinions, biases and assumptions that fall on top of clear knowing, essence and experience. You may want to bring people together or serve in areas where you can create the space for genuine, clear and beneficial conversations, actions and change. You have the gift of being able to bring authenticity, not only to an individual but to the experience and expression of a whole that generates true transformation.

When you think of purity, when you feel into having clear, unembellished, transparent and authentic solutions, opportunities and collaborations to uplift our world, what does this inspire in you?

Blessings

The Blessings of the Stream of Purity

May you recognize appreciation and receive the
blessings of the Stream of Purity.

May gracious and conscious alignment
awaken for you.

May the path, journey and the sacred
clear and light your way.

May the blessings be in harmony with you
in the fullest.

May you become an aligned vessel
for clear Divine relationship.

CHAPTER SIX:

The Stream of Honor

each step echoes across the endless skies
the sacred breath sighs tributes
this greatness and majesty held so dear
exists for all to see and all to be

The Stream of Honor

The Stream of Honor is a resonating relationship of Divine blessing, light and frequency that allows and creates a direct experience and recognition of the Divine in all things. This awakens deep knowing and appreciation. This stream reveals and creates a clear experience of Divine connection and opens the high vibrations of Divine recognition, humility and mutual appreciation.

When a person enters and resonates with the Stream of Honor, the true relationship of this Divine connection and experience, becomes whole. The Stream of Honor brings an immediate experience of the magnitude and preciousness of the Divine in the All. Those who have experienced the Stream of Honor are awakening, humble, joyful and feel true. They perceive, respect and appreciate more of their Divine connection and the resonance of the All.

The Invitation of the Stream of Honor

The Stream of Honor holds the energies of Honor. Honor is extended outward, as well as inward. Honor is an energetic loop which pours outward to another and reflects inward. The vibrational pattern circulates. It moves inward through a person's entire energy field, reorienting the aspects of disdain, derision and unworthiness. It moves outward, highlighting those same aspects and thought processes in the world to reorient them toward appreciation and inclusion. The amount of re-attunement from the Stream of Honor one can receive correlates to the amount of honor one can bestow upon one's self as a reflection of the Divine.

The Stream of Honor holds that every thought and deed is a reflection of the honor an individual accords to the Divine. How you treat your mother is a reflection of how you treat God. How you treat your animals is a reflection of how you treat God. How you treat the land is a reflection of how you treat God. How you treat a stranger is a reflection of how you treat God. How you treat yourself is a reflection of how you treat God. If you walk the path of Honor, you must look into the eyes of humanity and know that each person comes from the Divine and is an aspect of the Divine. They must be honored accordingly or you are defaming the sacred truth and teachings.

Imagine what your life would look like from the inside, if everything you did conferred honor, respect and appreciation. You expressed honor and respect to your family, to your land, to the salespeople in every store, to those you disagree with and to those you do not like or even admire. You do this simply because everything is a manifestation of the Divine in whatever form it presents itself. Therefore, every encounter you have in life is an opportunity to express your honor and recognition of the Divine. This is indeed profound.

The Invocation of the Stream of Honor

The energy patterns of the Stream of Honor circulate and expand in a loose vibrating web, connecting each and every aspect of being. This web is infinitely fine and in constant motion and flux. The pattern has its own structure which appears to be in continual change, yet is very specific in nature. When in concord with the Stream of Honor, one becomes part of this circular web. Inner expansion and recalibration to these distinct energies move inward into the core of personal being and then outward into the relatedness of all being. Honor creates a powerful relationship with the one (you) and the all (everything else) and the One (Divine) and the All (Totality).

The vibrational essence of the Stream of Honor travels in a circuit. It infuses the inner being and moves forward out into the world and the community. When a person is moving within the stream or being aligned with the Stream of Honor, then their inner nature, their emotions down to the soul level, is being realigned to understand honor in its Divine sense. To be honoring is a recognition and a clear appreciation of how the Divine moves in all things. Honor is active, as well as receptive, and includes the actions which ensue and are taken when one experiences the energies of honor.

This inner wisdom then moves through a person's entire system, and that person will vibrate to the frequencies and patterns of honor. Honor then becomes a way of experiencing the world and relating with the world. The patterns simultaneously shift from an inner experience to an outward extension of this honor to all of life. The cycle continues, in that, extending the honor outward to all living beings and to all of the gifts and challenges of life creates another level of honor that is ingested back into this same person.

To honor and to extend honor in all directions requires a singular focus and a supreme generosity of being. Since humanity is focused in this life, it is necessary to also consider one's own needs and desires.

Distinguishing the levels and subtleties of honor afford the opportunity to increase the extension of honor in the world. Through this understanding, you can move further into acknowledging and appreciating your own being. Through this distinction and recognition, you resonate more closely with Divine essence. Your own inner sense of honor in all that you are and all that you do creates a generous vibration of true Divine relatedness.

The Experience of the Stream of Honor

The Stream of Honor teaches the honoring of all people, all beings and all relationships as pathways to the Divine. To honor is to appreciate, revere, respect, acknowledge and extend accord to yourself, to another and to the Divine. The appreciation and recognition of the Divine within all beings creates a profound relatedness. Each aspect of life is vital. Each relationship is profound. Nothing can be taken for granted. No action, no thought, no communication is above or beyond direct relationship with the Divine. Therefore, every action, thought and communication is to convey honor. This brings forward a great humility and appreciation. The direct knowing of honor within the Divine awakens the experience of an equality amongst people, an appreciation of animals and land and the desire and accomplishment of many things created specifically to honor the Divine. This Stream brings forth a great intellect, through which the process of learning becomes a process of honoring the Divine wisdom that can be revealed through study.

The distinctions of honor and respect and acknowledgment are very clear and could even appear specific. This is the nature of the Stream of Honor. Highly defined levels of honor are highly defined vibrational patterns. To be in an expanding appreciation and sharing of these frequencies creates a sublime relatedness in which the honored and the one extending honor become whole, together. Honor is experienced by both. Honor is extended out into the Universal and showers upon the wholeness of creation.

Each stream aligns you with its own attunements and brings you to higher levels of spiritual awareness, wholeness, Divine connection and enlightenment. This is true of the Stream of Honor. For a person resonating with the frequencies of honor, extending honor to every aspect of life is a natural way to be. The joy and appreciation of the Divine is seen and experienced in every moment of existence, for every essence of existence. Each Stream of Consciousness brings you to the same joyous knowing of the Divine. Each stream differs in its alignments. Each stream can be encountered on its own.

The Stream of Honor extends to all. In the pathways of time, honor is consistent. Honor is the same. Honor cannot be translated or interpreted. The actions to confer honor may be interpreted, but the vibrational integrity of honor is consistent.

The Influences from the Stream of Honor

The energies, qualities and perspective arising from the Stream of Honor align with a deep respect and recognition of all life. You may feel a genuine appreciation for life. You may feel a sense of reverence and humility for the gifts that life and the Divine showers upon you and are held within this world. You may approach life and situations with the understanding that you honor each and every being and circumstance. This generates a relatedness that is a very even flow towards all people, nature and circumstances. You know that extending honor, respect and recognition is a gift that brings beauty to all.

How may the Stream of Honor influence your life?

Personal Vision inspired by the Stream of Honor

You may see your own life and the world as more than people can recognize. You may celebrate the unsung heroes and those who may go unnoticed. You may see and appreciate those who stand up for others or give without recognition or have generous spirits with all. You may be one who sees and recognizes the contribution, the effort, the inner alignment and the challenges people face that go unnoticed. You may wonder why others don't see or acknowledge these contributions. You see and feel and know the honoring spirit and the honor of the Divine within everyone. You are one to acknowledge people for who they are and what they do.

Relatedness inspired by the Stream of Honor

Relatedness within honor is a way granting accord or recognizing and celebrating the inner being and the outward living of a person or people. You look at relationships in a direct recognition of the whole person and the path of their life. You also feel honored to be part of genuine, true relatedness. In relationship this respect, consideration, esteem and integrity brings a truth, a trust and a recognition. People feel heard and known as you honor them. You honor their life, their work, their efforts and their own truth and service. This goes beyond service and outward expressions. You hold people in that honor, and they recognize how much you see, and how much you commend their lives.

You seek a way of honor so that all are appreciated and recognized. For some people extending honor to them may feel unwarranted or even aggrandizing. For you it is a true recognition of life and of the Divine within all life. You open a space of appreciation for all.

World View inspired by the Stream of Honor

Honor as a world view or cosmic view brings a profound sense of recognition. The brilliance, the creativity, the innovation, the effort, the perseverance, the contribution from all moves you greatly. You may seek out ways to share your appreciation and gratitude for the gifts and efforts from others. You may feel moved to find people who have not been recognized or situations that can benefit from acknowledgement and positive attention and shine some light upon their goodness and contributions.

When you think of honor, when you feel the truth of someone's life, challenges, efforts and the goodness of their soul, what does this inspire in you?

Blessings

The Blessings of the Stream of Honor

May you recognize, share and receive the blessings
of the Stream of Honor.

May you receive honor and grant yourself
honor in the flow of life.

May you resonate, breath and see
the honor of all and the honor of the All.

May you become a vessel
for Divine recognition and appreciation.

CHAPTER SEVEN:

The Stream of Compassion

as these eyes look into hearts there is no distance
inspired to bring love which circles the cosmos
moved by souls in sacred connection
to reflect the you in me and the me in you

The Stream of Compassion

The Stream of Compassion is an oscillating wave of Divine frequency that reveals a direct experience and recognition of the interconnection of all things in the Divine. This awakens and opens many profound vibrational levels of understanding, generosity and perception and creates a clear appreciation of the interconnection of all things in the Divine.

When a person enters and resonates with the Stream of Compassion, the true interrelatedness of this Divine and individual connection and its reverberations, generates understanding, empathy, kinship and humanity. The Stream of Compassion brings an immediate experience of the relatedness and reciprocity of the Divine in the All. Those who have experienced the Stream of Compassion are heartful, generous and feel genuine community. They know and celebrate their Divine connection with all beings and all life.

The Invitation of the Stream of Compassion

The Stream of Compassion is the expanding wisdom of understanding and empathy emanating from and in relationship to the Divine. This soft, expansive energy moves in waves from an inward experience to an outward relatedness. It encompasses the wisdom of knowing all things, all aspects of travel in the quest of knowing the Divine.

This soft flowing energy aligns the heart to a deep underanding and a compassion for all of the travels, experiences and awakenings that will bring one and attune one to the Divine Center of being. Through the connection and attunements of the Stream of Compassion one can feel the embrace of Divine magnitude in a personal expression of gentle knowing and acceptance. The vibrational emanations are soft and flowing. The experiences of moving in resonance to this stream can generate states of joy, bliss and profound understanding.

The Stream of Compassion holds the flow of specific qualities which uplift and expand human awareness of the Divine flow in all matters, things and relationships. It contains consideration, thoughtfulness, kindness and good will. Compassion is the state of being which holds shared understanding. What has occurred is known and felt, together. What has been experienced is known and felt in a union of being. What has been deeply felt is seen and known for its wholeness and in its relationship among individuals, to all beings everywhere and to the quest for Divine union. In this understanding and genuine extension and appreciation, kindness flows and good will is imparted.

The Stream of Compassion generates and expresses recognition. Initially, these qualities or states of awareness are experienced from connection with the Divine essence of compassion, of shared unity and embrace. As the initial expressions of these qualities move from the recognition of the Divine, they register and are held as qualities experienced with and shared with all of creation. The sacred relatedness of each being in its divinity is cherished. The simple truths and life experiences of each person are admired. Imagine the trials of your own life. You have been through pains and difficulties. Perhaps they seemed insurmountable at the time. These circumstances tested your endurance and strength and emotional balance. Deep emotions were present. Your struggles in that time, your challenges to overcome and resolve were paramount to your being and your life. The vibrational patterns of the Stream of Compassion would cherish you for the effort and strength that you expressed in these moments. A person resonating with this stream would naturally admire the effort and qualities and growth it took to move forward in those times. They would feel for you and with you. They would be in a shared relatedness with you. Knowing and feeling your life, and knowing and feeling all life, would show them the magnitude of your being, your challenge and your beauty in moving forward as you did. Your true value of being would be known and shared and admired for all that you are and all that you are becoming.

The Stream of Compassion contains reverence. This aspect of the quality of reverence is based in the connection to the Divine as a revered and admired essence. Through this direct knowing of the deep compassion of the Divine for every aspect of creation, reverence is expressed for all. The sacred is revered and through that admiration, all of life is held sacred. There is deference in reverence. One defers to the Divine in all things and notices this Divine in all people and in all of creation. The magnitude of the Divine reveals the diminutive stance of an individual. In this small and uplifted state, one knows the vast horizon of consciousness and in comparison, one is small. Yet this comparison also shows that the Divine nature and essence is within every aspect of being. It shows that you are filled with all of the beauty and glory of the Divine. As you defer to the greatness of the Divine, you are deferring to your own Divine nature and greatness. As you revere the Divine, you are in reverence to the Divine moving within you.

The Stream of Compassion contains forgiveness. Through all of these qualities and states of being, forgiveness is present. Understanding and having compassion for the experiences, choices, decisions and circumstances of another person's life, generates eternally flowing forgiveness. When compassion is present and the truth of being is known, forgiveness flows in all directions. The softness of spirit washes through the restrictions and bathes clear light into being.

Forgiveness flows from compassion. Compassion is experienced through relatedness. The frequencies of the Stream of Compassion send compassion, which washes away the burden to clear a new path of being. The new path of being reveals the traits and circumstances that can be healed. This healing, as well, can contain resolutions, actions and compensation. As compassion flows through each and all, restitution is a natural and healing revelation and act. Through the qualities and actions of forgiveness, true compensation for any harm can flow freely and heal both sides. This is the true and natural state of compassion.

The Invocation of the Stream of Compassion

The vibrational vortex of the Stream of Compassion resonates in series of waves that continually reveal related connections. Each wave opens a view or understanding or knowing in a series of pulses that illuminate a profound interrelatedness of being. One can experience a vibrational knowing of how thoughts, events and actions move an individual and the All. The flows of energies all reveal the beauty, the possibility and the true interwoven life of the Divine and the individual. One experiences a deep knowing that each moment, each being, each action influences each other and the all.

A person or being traveling in the Stream of Compassion experiences as these flows. This begins an awareness and recognition of the inherent connection that is woven into the nature of all life. The patterns of influence, of relatedness, from one instance in the flow of light to a distant galaxy to the sparkles of a sunrise on the ocean on earth become a knowing.

Vibrationally this has the similarity to a kaleidoscope of patterns. Each color or gem may appear separate and each has a relationship and connection to the full pattern that is also moving and changing. The experience of each color and motion, and the full changing pattern brings an understanding of influence and connection. This gives a deeper, greater and true understanding, affinity, communion, sensitivity and sense of humanity.

The Stream of Compassion is a specific resonance that uplifts an individual through the bounty of understanding and community knowing. It is a shared perspective. Compassion is an aspect of relatedness. One cannot have compassion without another individual involved in relationship.

The Stream of Compassion resonates with consideration, kindness and good will. This state of shared understanding is continually present within the energies and vibrations of the stream. Anyone who wishes to experience this special union of being can move in concord with the Stream of Compassion and experience that energy.

The Experience of the Stream of Compassion

The Stream of Compassion flows in a synchronistic manner. Once the stream's qualities begin to infuse within an individual, there is an outpouring of compassion in the world. Each encounter, experience and alignment to that encounter and to the energies of the stream, flows naturally within and then naturally into the world and beyond.

The Stream of Compassion holds and imbues many qualities that generate enormous gifts for understanding and healings. Encountering the Stream of Compassion once, does not completely alter a person's being and bring instant enlightenment. However, it does impart its essence and qualities. One encounter with the Stream of Compassion can bring forth greater wisdom and emotional generosity.

Each dominant expression of a Stream of Consciousness directs you to experience an aspect of the Divine. Each Stream of Consciousness holds and vibrates to specific spiritual qualities which are aspects of the Divine. That aspect of the Divine can lead you to experience an epiphany of spiritual awakening. This epiphany gives you access to attunements which can lead to many levels of awakening and enlightenment. The Stream of Compassion leads to illumination through the attunements and wisdom of compassion, thoughtfulness and relationship inherent in Divine communication.

Every stream is an avenue toward enlightenment. Every stream gives you access to wisdom, harmony, joy and communion with the Divine. No one stream is better than another. No one stream has greater access to the Divine than another. This is also a revelation and wisdom of The Stream of Compassion. The Stream of Compassion holds and resonates to deep understanding and connection with all people, all life. This quality and vibrational pathway will call to certain individuals. "All roads lead to Home." The Stream of Compassion can bring new levels of blessing into the world.

The Influences from the Stream of Compassion

The energies, qualities, unique perspective and frequencies from the Stream of Compassion influence one's life in a very intimate way. You feel and know. You sense and relate. You open in recognition and extend your heart, your connection and your knowing. You may sense another's life and feel what is asking to be known. You may notice on a deeper level that which calls out to be created, uplifted, changed and admired. You may wonder why others may not recognize or will simply ignore the needs or longings of others, because to you they are so evident. You can feel the beauty in each being and the flow lightens your heart.

How may the Stream of Compassion influence your life?

Personal Vision inspired by the Stream of Compassion

You may see the world as an interrelated experience. You may, at times, feel a deep resonance and communication with people, beings, places and events. You know deeply that all are related. You may feel empathic as your connection with life is deeply personal. You may wonder at the beauty and richness and courage of people, that most others may not even notice. You feel the connection with all life. You may focus on certain people or areas where you know appreciation, kindness and good will is wanted.

Relatedness inspired by the Stream of Compassion

Relatedness within Compassion is a dance of recognition, celebration and knowing. You know that you are part of the life and all life and this is meaningful and moving. You feel interconnection and relationship as a heartfelt calling and appreciation of that person or people or beings. You look at relationships from the outside in and the inside out, seeing the loop of understanding, connection, caring and appreciation all flowing in a sacred silence. You have compassion for a person's life, dreams, growth and presence. This goes beyond your chosen partner or family. You feel and know that bond with all and you feel gratitude and reverence for this knowing.

You seek a way of compassion so that all people, animals, beings, land and situations are appreciated and valued. For some people resonating with compassion feels like love and love for all. You appreciate, understand and celebrate all of life and the Divine within all life. You share a space of love and understanding for all.

World View inspired by the Stream of Compassion

Compassion in a world view or cosmic view reveals an open heart that wants to help uplift the world. Your powerful connection with all life is personal and this moves you to contribute in many different ways. You may create opportunities for others to help others and open more compassion in the world. You may sense that helping certain people will create a shift that changes their lives. You may feel that relatedness to all life and help people develop connection and community that is intimate, caring and accepting.

When you think of compassion, when you explore creating relatedness, resolutions and possibilities to uplift our world through compassion, what does this inspire in you?

Blessings

The Blessings of the Stream of Compassion

May you open to the flows of compassion, love and relatedness in this world.

May you receive heartfelt consideration, thoughtfulness, kindness and good will.

May you see, know, feel and participate in interconnected, interrelated, shared understanding.

May you become a vessel for Divine interrelatedness and understanding.

CHAPTER EIGHT:

The Stream of Neutrality

crystal reflections shine in translucent wisdom
sending meaningful messages in context
all equal, liberated, valued, knowing, seen and felt
noticed, appreciated and present in suchness

The Stream of Neutrality

The Stream of Neutrality is a centralizing focus of Divine frequency that reveals an interrelated recognition of all things in the Divine. This reveals systemic vibrational levels throughout all creation to hold profound understanding and alliance of the interconnection and value of all things in the Divine.

When a person enters and resonates with the Stream of Neutrality, the true clarity of each aspect of the Divine and creation is revealed. The Stream of Neutrality brings an immediate experience of the relatedness, interdependence and reciprocity of the Divine in the All. Those who have experienced the Stream of Neutrality are radiant, positive and feel connected. They know, feel and cherish the importance of all beings and all life.

The Invitation of the Stream of Neutrality

The Stream of Neutrality is a focus of centeredness. The energies of this stream provide a view of the interrelatedness of all things as aspects of the Divine. Within the neutrality of this vibrational pattern, each life and consciousness is as important as another. The relativity of space and size do not constitute any level of importance or dominance. As all is important and all is Divine, there is no specific emotional attachment to which is better, more right or more evolved. All is in perfection. Perfection is the nature of being.

Neutrality, in its essence, is the awareness of the whole without polarity. It is an avenue through which the Divine reveals itself as an essence of experience. Neutrality strips away desire and judgment to reveal the essence of spirit in all of its glory and harmony. It reveals and expresses the harmony of the All.

The Stream of Neutrality is an omni-focused experience. Vibrationally, as one moves in resonance with the stream, a singular point of reference becomes more diffused or less personal. Viewing oneself as part of the whole of creation, the whole of creation becomes part of oneself. It is in this relationship with the Divine All, that awakening reveals itself. As the levels of appreciation grow, perceptions expand. A personal life view is present, yet it is present within the wholeness of creation. For the most part, separation ceases to exist. Resonating in harmony with the Stream of Neutrality avails a perspective and knowing of the whole, which is within one's own being and extends beyond one's own field of knowing. Even that which is beyond touch, beyond experience and beyond recognition, is within one's own being. The Divine is within one's own being. An ant, a tree, a black hole, the unified field is all within one's own being. The shapes and forms have nothing to do with importance or degree. The shapes and forms of creation are containers for the Divine.

All Streams of Consciousness reorganize one's persptive. Each has a specific vibrational pattern which shapes the experience of this reorganization. The Stream of Neutrality does so from an intimate and personal perspective or focus, by a comparison or relative point of reference. As the mind becomes more quiet, it is filled with the space of the Divine. The Stream of Neutrality reorganizes personal perspective in a series of attunements to realign the individual view into a more encompassing view. It is a point and counterpoint approach to recognizing the Divine in all things.

One stands on top of the mountain and sees the view of the valley below and the sky above. The focus shifts within. One now stands in the valley and sees the mountain above and the sky above that. The focus shifts within again, one views the mountain below and the valley below that as alternate views of a greater view of being. No one landscape is better than another. No one position is more sacred. The sky is not less than the mountain. The valley is not less than the sky. This position of understanding opens a calm relatedness within the individual. All is related. All is Divine. All is a unique vista of the magnitude and intimacy of the Divine essence of creation. All is Divine and this is the only perspective available.

The Invocation of the Stream of Neutrality

The energy patterns of the Stream of Neutrality move to single out similarities of being. The vibrational point of reference from the individual has a compatible resonance to another essence or aspect of creation. Both are triggered to vibrate at the same time, which infuses the individual with the recognition that this resonance permeates another aspect of being or many aspects of being. Similarity is felt and perceived. The individual's view point shifts in resonance from their normal view to the view of the other, which is resonating at the same frequency. The individual is availed of another position which is similar to their own. Interrelatedness is revealed in an instant. Like finds like. Like resonates to like. Like views existence from within the position of the other. The individual view expands in relationship to all other like resonances. Otherness dissolves into relatedness. There is no other. All is.

The Stream of Neutrality gives an individual the opporunity to merge with the Divine from recognition of their illusion of polarity and separation. It holds the unique vibrational standpoints, the individual view points, and uses them to reveal the interrelatedness of all things, all perspectives and all views. Each separate view is an honorable one. Each separate view reveals the totality. By explicitly using the separation or polarities of these stands and positions, unity and wholeness become accessible. As every aspect is resonating to the same frequency and one can be within all separate containers of that frequency and see from that perspective, then the boundaries are loosened and the Divine is revealed within each position. Separation becomes the tool of Oneness.

Each Stream of Consciousness brings new aspects of Divine spirit into life in a more specified way. The Stream of Neutrality can feel or appear balanced, whole and serene. The frequencies of neutrality resonate to the center point of any given experience. The center point of resonance between love and hate is understanding. The center point between good and bad is perception. The center point between right and wrong is appropriateness. The relativity of each polarized view is not a fixed position. One can perceive variations of good and bad. One can perceive degrees of right and wrong. Yet, between even the most subtle degrees of polarity is a position or vibration of neutrality.

Recognition or experience of the Stream of Neutrality can and does generate advanced degrees of spiritual enlightenment. This is so of any Stream, since the nature of a Stream is to awaken the individual to the totality of the Divine in all aspects of life. Personal experience of the Stream of Neutrality in a mode of advanced participation, generates relatedness to the All and the One in smooth recognition. The pathway within the stream may show states of bliss or despair, but the resulting attunements carry serenity, recognition and relatedness. Clarity of mind, vision and purpose is shown and experienced.

The Experience of the Stream of Neutrality

The Stream of Neutrality reveals the spirit of each in the All. You can look into another's eyes and see the Divine. You can look at a flower and see the Divine. The same experience is present in each. This understanding of and participation with the Stream of Neutrality opens a dialogue with all beings and all consciousness. It is a position of strong relationship.

Through the Stream of Neutrality and the resonance of its specific energies, you can feel and know the Divine presence in all beings as an equal Divine expression. The joy and accomplishment of another creates joy within oneself, because the brilliance and beauty of the Divine is moving within the joy. It becomes evident through that person and experience. It shines upon you because you noticed it. It is a revelation of the presence of spirit to you from another. That individual, who revealed their joy to you, has shined that joy into your life. Their joy expands your joy. From this deeper connection, the joy contributes to your joy and to the joy of all beings everywhere. It becomes a profound truth and blessing for all. There is no comparative view of whose joy is better, or whose life is better. The perfection of the Divine is revealed.

Each person's experience becomes an avenue for Divine revelation. It becomes a vehicle for experiencing the One and the All. Life expands through this participation. One person's method becomes a contribution to the whole of being. A higher understanding is achieved, because you recognize that there is a higher understanding to achieve. Personal spiritual resonance or group spiritual resonance will flow toward that higher understanding as a matter of course. Guided by the Stream of Neutrality, in the presence of this person, you move from recognition into relatedness and from relatedness into joyous appreciation. There is no judgment as in good or bad. There is an understanding of higher levels of experience which are reflected in the knowing that all life and all experience is a woven relatedness of the Divine All.

The revelations of the Stream of Neutrality bring a deeper balance and appreciation to the individual participating with it. The exquisite flow of Divine nature and purpose and relatedness brings wisdom and graciousness. Through this knowing and experience a greater ease of being unfolds. The cares of another are clear and evident, which can lead to a solving of problems in a more respectful and appreciative manner. The Stream of Neutrality motivates the actions taken by an individual in resonance with stream. Being in a place of understanding and regard for each individual of creation, the person can find the highest resolution to a specific problem or event.

Choices are always made. Choices are made every instant of life. Through those choices you reveal yourself to yourself. Every stream of spiritual energy and every one of the Streams of Consciousness is elegant, beautiful and Divinely lit. Each has specific attunements within it that provide a unique Divine perspective. The Stream of Neutrality brings an equanimity, a grace and appreciation of all beings. All life and all wisdom are an honored and vital part of the Divine.

The Stream of Neutrality is an unbiased understanding of Divine experience. Through this resonance of Divine relatedness, meditation is as important as personal affairs. How you treat the Divine is as important as how you treat another person. In fact, they are specifically and unrefutably related.

When you are attracted to and participating with the Stream of Neutrality, you can see the effects of the actions about to be taken. Then from this perspective, the most appropriate actions will be taken. These actions are appropriate from the stance of Divine connection. They are not specifically judged good or bad. They are deemed appropriate because they are in keeping with Divine flow in the individual and those involved. No harm shall come from this view and its ensuing actions. Each thought and position is important, not more important or less important. Each is equally important. It is a flow of quietude, filling all aspects of consciousness with appreciation and recognition of the Divine in all things. Through this knowing and deep experience, a person finds the way to be present in the Divine harmony of being, no matter which actions must be taken.

Using the Stream of Neutrality as a reference point, no experience of the Divine is more than or less than another. One person's epiphany is not better than another's. Each is founded in the experience of the individual connecting to higher aspects and awarenesses of spirituality. In this regard, encountering the Stream of Neutrality or seeking it as a way of experiencing the Divine would be as desirable as seeking any other Stream or no Stream at all. Coming from the direct perspective of the Stream of Neutrality, all spiritual experience is in perfection and equally profound and desirable. What you choose to follow is more specifically related to individual preference, personal and soul focus, and personality make-up. This is the brilliance of the Stream of Neutrality.

The Influences from the Stream of Neutrality

The energies, qualities and greater view from the Stream of Neutrality bring a clarity of reference wherein the brilliance, importance and contribution of all and the one are equally considered. You may feel the wisdom contained within each person as an equal and valuable contribution to your world. You may see all peoples, all animals, nature and beings as separate and equal in the eyes of the Divine and in your eyes, too. You may feel the excitement of discovery when a new and different idea or way of being is presented, as you perceive the interrelatedness of everything. You may wonder why so many people favor preference and do not realize the equal brilliance of all. You know in your being that the totality celebrates individual brilliance in everything.

How may the Stream of Neutrality influence your life?

Personal Vision inspired by the Stream of Neutrality

You may experience the world as an interrelated flow of many pieces and beings all contributing to the wholeness and quality of life. You may notice the individual pieces and recognize the value of specific aspects, and you also recognize the value of all. As you experience Neutrality, you have an openness an equanimity and appreciation of all people and perspectives, and that excites you. You celebrate the differences as contributions and opportunities for understanding and growth. You appreciate the contrast and counterpoints and are free and unbiased as to how the best will unfold. Your Personal Vision inspired by the Stream of Neutrality brings you curiosity and intrigue to experience the revelation of each individual piece and its importance to the whole.

Relatedness inspired by the Stream of Neutrality

Relatedness with Neutrality brings an open view that celebrates each unique aspect and wants to know more. You participate in relationships from an understanding or equal contribution, knowing that one person or one group is as important as the other. You feel and see the interplay of people as revelation of new aspects that are compatible in the highest ways. You look at relationships from a balance and serenity that allows for and encourages differences and unique perspectives. You are an open space of listening, hearing on the deepest levels and conferring related wisdom and honoring each separate view as important to the whole. You family and friends may feel you are the peacemaker, when you are in truth, being the open space where all are valued and heard.

You seek a way of neutrality so that all people and thoughts and views know their unique importance and their part in the whole. For some people this is a quiet, knowing space where people can truly be themselves and are liberated as well and considered valuable. You understand the truth and value of the interrelatedness of all things and casually shine that divinely held perspective.

World View inspired by the Stream of Neutrality

Neutrality in a world view or cosmic view comes from a place of peace, acceptance and listening. Your place of clarity and calm soothes the energy and discourse. You may be inspired to take leadership roles to unveil potential that is as yet unseen. You may create teachings and trainings where a centered perspective shines and helps people move to greater appreciation and considerate community. Neutrality in a global perspective and with global actions brings a togetherness where everyone and every opinion is valued, and opportunities for new perspectives are encouraged.

When you think of neutrality, when you look at bringing interrelatedness, connection and peaceful possibilities to uplift our world through neutrality, what does this inspire in you?

Blessings

The Blessings of the Stream of Neutrality

May you flow with the reverence of
interconnectedness and value of
all things in the Divine.

May you gain perspective and knowing of the
whole, and its existence in your own being.

May you live free to know the essence, value and
wisdom of spirit in all of its glory and harmony.

May you become a vessel for Divine mutuality,
equality and symmetry.

CHAPTER NINE:

The Stream of Harmony

many tones, countless blessings
roll into a chorus of synchronicity
voices of awakening
converge into infinite, melodious oneness in
concert

The Stream of Harmony

The Stream of Harmony is a multi-focused chamber of Divine frequency that reveals an interrelated collaboration of all things in the Divine. It is an individual and collective participation throughout all creation to celebrate individual personal expression and the cooperative participation of all things in the Divine.

When a person enters and resonates with the Stream of Harmony, the brilliance of the Divine and the brilliance of each aspect of creation becomes distinctly whole. The Stream of Harmony brings an immediate experience of relatedness, collaboration and synchronicity with life. Those who have experienced the Stream of Harmony are buoyant, hopeful and feel connected.

The Invitation of the Stream of Harmony

Harmony is a recognition, appreciation and awareness of each specific aspect of life in relationship to all life. It is a knowing of the interrelatedness of all beings, all situations and all portions of the Divine as a collaborative expression. Harmony is the interweaving of different and unique aspects into a congruent and singular arrangement. The Stream of Harmony is a specific vibratory resonance that exposes and expresses this Divine arrangement.

The Stream of Harmony is a recognition of Divine collaboration. Each part of creation, each particle of being is a resonant expression of the sacred moving in harmonious relationship to and within the All. Each individual voice blends together to a greater form. Each gift, tempo of life and strength contributes to the wholeness of being. The voices of the stars sing with the voices of the crickets and the calls of the coyotes. There is a rhythm and a melody to all creation and a rhythm and melody that unifies all creation. This is the vibratory pattern of the Stream of Harmony.

The Invocation of the Stream of Harmony

The Stream of Harmony creates the vibratory opening for variety and accord. This is the vibratory pattern of the stream. This stream of many frequencies resonates in multiple ways and patterns all held in a synchronous flow. The individual resonances shine and reveal the complementary connections that reveal groupings and timings that become patterns of revelation and participation. In this sacred flowing and knowing, the singular and infinite move to express diversity, blend to become a collection and shine to the multiplicity. The Stream of Harmony always creates harmony in ways that are continually changing.

The pathway is created by an opening that continues to expand and adapt to countless experiences, and while doing so, creates a harmonious relationship amongst all of those experiences. The fullness of each expression, each nuance and understanding is given space to fulfill itself within the context of wholeness. As each essence of being, whether that is an experience or a consciousness, moves into the stream, the opening for its relationship with itself and all others present is expanded and attuned. The stream creates an expansive appreciation and recognition of the individuality that is held within the wholeness. Each aspect has its celebrated place and relationship within the whole.

In the Stream of Harmony, nothing is isolated from the Divine. Everything holds the presence of the Divine and is a sacred reflection and a sacred teaching. Each being, mineral, plant, animal, human or particle has a life of its own which contributes to and enhances all of life in all of time. Each one is sacred in its own right and each one is equally sacred through its relationship to every other individual and group presence.

Living life from this wisdom reveals a flow of beauty and power within the Divine. It reveals the beauty and importance of each individual life, for its selfhood and for the contribution that its life gives to the wholeness. The vibratory patterns of creation are shown in their higher aspects through the magnificent interrelatedness that is evident in the vibration and is held in the space between individual and the All. This is the space of harmony.

The Experience of the Stream of Harmony

The Stream of Harmony expresses the magnificent interrelationships of all life, to every particle of being. Harmony acknowledges and appreciates individual gifts and talents. It holds these gifts as vital to the overall harmony and creativity of Divine essence, expression and life. Through the individual's qualities, the Divine can paint a larger painting of the wonders of it all. Individual expression is subjective.

Deciding which is an individual and which is part of something else is subjective. The air moving outside of you is the wind. The air moving inside of you is the breath. When does the wind become the breath? When does the breath become the wind? At what instant are they changed?

The wind generates the breath and is in harmony with it. It provides the space for breathing. Yet, the breath returns to the wind and once again becomes part of it. Are you breathing the breaths of billions of life forms throughout time? Are you breathing the winds of ancient earth times? You breathe it all, wind and breath, in a harmony of living. Your breath contributes to the flow of the winds and the breaths of all beings. The winds contribute to the flow of all air which is breathed back into itself. This is the Stream of Harmony.

The revelation and experience of harmony can easily be seen in choir music. Each person in the choir has their musical range, the notes which can be sung clearly and comfortably. Each person in the choir is chosen for their qualities and voice. They receive the music, the parts to be sung. Some of the voices are higher, some are lower. The music reflects these differences in voices, notes, tempo and volume to create a wholeness in the musical piece to be sung. The singers come into the song at different levels and often at different times. Some voices reach high notes, others hold the melody and some sing the lowest notes in the music. The harmony they achieve occurs with the blending of all of these voices into a beautiful wholeness that swells with sound.

A single voice cannot sing harmony. Harmony requires a collective collaboration. Several voices singing the same part do not create harmony. The harmony occurs when each voice moves in relationship to the other voices, feeling into the qualities and strengths of all the voices and blending the individual voice with the wholeness. When that occurs, harmony is present.

As in musical harmony, the beauty is a joining of voices into a collective wholeness. The harmony happens in the wholeness. The harmony happens in the space provided for the individual voices merging into relatedness. Harmony is created in the space and revealed in the relationships within that space. It is not a singular event. Harmony is a revelation of appreciation unfolding through time.

All aspects of creation are honored contributions to life. They generate and reveal a harmonious and sacred wholeness. This world reveals and celebrates harmony. The mountains reveal the majesty of being and the valley below shows its fullness. Each complements the other. Would the mountain be as high without the valley below? Would the valley below be as lush and serene without the mountain rising above it? Both reflect a harmonious wholeness of place.

You are part of this totality, of this living system, which is in harmony with itself and with all beings. This Harmony extends beyond what is seen and what is known and opens the Stream of Harmony so you may consciously be a harmonious flow of life, in life and for life.

The Influences from the Stream of Harmony

The energies, qualities and unique perspective from the Stream of Harmony influence one's life in a melodic way. You may feel inspired by many different aspects of being. You may love nature and want to immerse yourself within it and see all of life in a fullness. You may celebrate the richness of diversity in your own life and in this world. You may wonder at the profound richness that many people do not even see, because you can see the many in the one. You can feel the contribution of alignment that makes all things shine in their brilliance, together.

How may the Stream of Harmony influence your life?

Personal Vision inspired by the Stream of Harmony

You may see the world and see your life as many parts that create a wholeness. You may, at times, feel the parts as separate, and you know the separate parts create the whole of you. You have many talents and perspectives. You move to combine them in a harmony, a richness that encourages all of your gifts to flow together. You celebrate the eclectic. You embrace many things and know that all of it contributes to your life. Your Personal Vision inspired by the Stream of Harmony brings you to many different experiences and situations, that allow you to blend, and expand and celebrate the many. You can feel how it all comes together in appreciation of each voice, each idea, each expression. All of this inspires and excites you.

You know that harmony asks a special focus. You have a special gift of being able to see beyond an individual point of view and expand your vision to appreciative inclusivity.

Relatedness inspired by the Stream of Harmony
Relatedness is part of harmony. One note is distinct and reveals the other note is also distinct, and yet they create something new and beautiful, sounding together. In your relationships with individuals, you are looking for that harmonious connection. You look to contribution with a focus of getting along. Whether in your personal relationships or in your community relationships, you look to acknowledge each other and celebrate the unique qualities that each person brings. You appreciate unique qualities, gifts and perspectives and can truly see how that can contribute and open new possibilities, new alliances and new interpersonal connections that may not have happened without the influence of the harmony.

You seek a way of harmony to bring everything together in ways that recognize the special and individual ways of thinking and being, and how they all can contribute to more for everyone. This creates a very unique experience. Listening to each individual expression, hearing the differences and opening a space for all to be heard and to play together.

World View inspired by the Stream of Harmony
Harmony in a world view or cosmic view reveals so many opportunities to collaborate, celebrate and appreciate. You

may seek out ways to contribute by bringing people together in a focus that helps them relate to each other and create true community. You may have dreams that bring resources to others or create solutions that recognize the differences of location, ideology and understanding and you look to creating the help that harmoniously fits into that location, ideology and understanding.

When you think of harmony, when you feel into having harmonious solutions, opportunities and collaborations to uplift our world, what does this inspire in you?

Blessings

The Blessings of the Stream of Harmony

May you feel and know the interrelatedness
of all beings as a collaborative expression.

May you celebrate the interweaving of individual
aspects into a congruous and singular arrangement.

May you know the vibratory resonance
that expresses this Divine arrangement of infinite
variety and participation.

May you become a vessel for Divine
diversity and collaboration.

CHAPTER TEN:

The Stream of Beauty and Grace

moments, presence, benevolent peace
sighs speak in abundant splendor
stars, petals, particles, smiles all sparkle
in quiet resonance revealing the exquisite presence

The Stream of Beauty and Grace

The Stream of Beauty and Grace is a dual reflection of Divine revelation that inspired each aspect to become more. These frequencies illuminate, inspire and focus on Divine brilliance outwardly and inwardly to engage and celebrate the majesty, in which high spiritual qualities are manifest.

When a person enters and resonates with the Stream of Beauty and Grace, the pleasure, elegance and revelation of the Divine and Divine creation becomes personal and real. The Stream of Beauty and Grace brings an evolving experience of recognition and appreciation. Those who have experienced the Stream of

Beauty and Grace are moved and inspired. They perceive the beauty and grace of the Divine with a presence and reflection of the All.

The Invitation of the Stream of Beauty and Grace

The Stream of Beauty and Grace is an entwining reflection of the miraculous. Its resonance reaches into each particle enhancing and smoothing a new state of being and appreciation in the Stream of Beauty and Grace. Endless vibratory patterns are expressed in their optimal combinations to reflect a majestic significator of the Divine. Beauty is inspirational and Grace is the reflection of that beauty extended outward while received inward. Grace is the revelation of beauty infused and ingested into one's being. Beauty is the revelation of Divine expression's flowing grace. Beauty and Grace flow together.

Beauty also moves as an outer flow, a recognition of something inspirational outside of one's self that triggers appreciation, awe and delight. One sees or feels or recognizes beauty as a perception, and then an opening of the appreciation is initiated. A flower, snow on the mountain tops, stars across an evening sky, a color, a strain of music, a child's laughter, the shimmer of fur, the colors of a rainbow, your lover's eyes, your friend's voice, the sound of the wind through the trees, each and all of these can inspire the recognition of beauty.

Grace moves as an inner energy flow, appearing to come from outside to illuminate a vibration of delicate generosity which triggers an immediate opening for receiving. Vibrationally, one appears to receive grace. Specifically, one opens to the flows of grace and resonates to that energy in a harmonious appreciation. In this opening or recognition, personal frequency moves into resonance with the grace that is a constant universal flow. The energies, spiritually, are soft, fluid, silent and embracing. The energies when felt can be inspirational, powerful, releasing and transformational.

The Invocation of the Stream of Beauty and Grace

The Stream of Beauty and Grace resonates as a vibratory focus of complement and reflection. One vibrational attunement sounds and becomes the forward motion of attention. The other vibrational frequency oscillates and brings attention to its sympathetic reverberation. Each vibration sounds and moves to pulsate a knowing and relationship that awakens and shines a new light into the world and into beingness. This is an interweaving of perception and reception that creates continual awakening, appreciation, inspiration and feelings of awe and wonder. Each aspect, each vibration and revelation of Beauty and Grace, introduces, highlights and proclaims each other in a continuing enhancement and expansion of Divine recognition.

Beauty and Grace resonate together as a unity in which each aspect has its own distinctive revelation. While resonating to and within the Stream of Beauty and Grace, one may perceive a specific aspect in greater distinction than the another, yet both are specifically entwined. One may notice beauty and not be aware that grace is present. One may experience grace and not recognize beauty's appearance. And while beauty and grace appear to be outside, meaning that they are viewed from an individual perception looking or feeling out into the world, in that same instant, the qualities of their resonance activate an inhalation of the energies. One breathes in grace. One breathes in beauty. Therefore, in recognition of grace and beauty, one is filled with grace and beauty. The flowing celebration of Divine perfection is inhaled and moving within the "viewer." One participates and becomes beauty and grace by one's recognition of beauty and grace.

In the in-flowing of the Stream of Beauty and Grace, one can hold these energies and resonate to these energies. In doing so, one is the revelation of beauty and grace. A perfect example of this is a ballet dancer. Her movements are fluid. Each turn of the hand, curve of the body, leap into the air, is grace embodied. The graceful and grace-filled movements are within that dancer. She is holding and revealing grace in her performance. As grace is revealed, so is beauty. It is impossible to imagine the dancer without feeling beauty. There is an elegant expression of beauty held and vibrating within the grace of body in motion. Grace and beauty are entwined. The viewer sees this, feels this as they watch. The dancer embodies these entwined energies and qualities within. The dancer evokes the Stream of Beauty and Grace as she performs and engages the audience in this expression within which she is reveling. The audience then, becomes a part of this expression. They are held within grace and beauty. The audience breathes it in. Their bodies become containers of grace and beauty. When the performance is complete and the audience leaves the theater, they move differently. They are more aware of the fluidity of their own motions, their balance. They are held within the expression and resonating to it.

The Experience of the Stream of Beauty and Grace

Grace and beauty ask for participation. That which is revealed in its splendor, asks for recognition in the beholder. The beholder is bathed in beauty and grace, through which they are integral parts and participants of beauty and grace. These finely tuned vibratory patterns of awareness flow, weave and resonate to greater openings and perceptions. You, the viewer or experiencer of the beauty, are entwined within the energies and vibratory patterns of beauty. Grace flows within these vibratory patterns. It moves and swirls within the resonance of beauty and stimulates your own beauty. This opens your recognition of beauty which expands the resonance of beauty in greater fullness. The energies of grace, flowing within the beauty matrix, enhance and augment the recognition and receiving of the energies of beauty.

At the same time the vibratory patterns of grace are flowing within beauty, the patterns of beauty are flowing within the energies of grace. As the frequencies of grace awaken the expansion and reception of Divine delight and creation, the opening for beauty is revealed. Each aspect is fluid. It is a rolling energy, like dolphins at play, flocks of birds curving in flight, the sway of weeping willow branches in the wind. While it appears evident that you may perceive beauty as an outer revelation that initiates an open response, you can also perceive grace as the fluidity of beauty. The perceptions of grace and beauty bring a resonance, a vibratory pattern of awakening which is held and experienced as appreciation. This is not merely an outer appreciation for what is revealed, but an inner appreciation of what is known and therefore felt. It is a living expression of the Divine displayed in splendor. Whether this splendor is subtle or grand, the frequencies and vibrational patterns of this energy holds an epiphany and recognition of a relationship with the Divine.

The Stream of Beauty and Grace is a direct pathway of expression and relationship with Divine Source. Personal life views, cultural views, social relatedness and global perspectives evolve based on the qualities and energies which elicit and celebrate beauty and grace.

Creating beauty, expressing beauty and relishing beauty is worshipful. It is a harmonious resonance with the Divine All that brings an individual into a higher consciousness, a spiritual recognition and participation with the Divine. It is beauty as communion. It is grace as spiritual revelation. Each aspect, which in actuality is a unit, brings the individual and the global perspective into a higher vibrational resonance and spiritual recognition. This is an awareness of the Divine that flows in all things, in all aspects. The mysterious is revealed through beauty and grace. Through being held and by holding the resonance and expression of beauty and grace, those energies are extolled. They are awakened and celebrated. This fluid revelation of the Divine shown in the Stream of Beauty and Grace, is a prayerful celebration of the beauty and grace of the Divine. The beauty and grace of the universe, the beauty and grace of all things and beings is a relationship and expression of the Divine flow that is everywhere, in all things and in all times, and in one moment. This is expressed and revered in the daily life and moments of the individual and culture.

The qualities of the Stream of Beauty and Grace reflect harmony, appreciation, recognition and delight. Inspiration is a natural state. To exemplify beauty, you hold and nurture inspiration. There is delight in every new leaf, every bouquet of flowers, every graceful curve of the hand. They are living expressions of the Divine, shown in another unique way. Beauty and grace are in motion and in change. These effects are living representations of the Divine.

Is this not how beauty and grace display their splendor? Is this not how the Divine reveals Herself, in every minute detail and combination of the universe?

As the individual and the culture are ensconced in the flow of the Stream of Beauty and Grace, the Divine is in constant revelation and relationship. Participation within the energies and vibrations of the stream brings a heightened sense, understanding and expression of the splendor of the All and the One. The focus is internal, external and interrelated. The curving fluid flow expresses and communicates. It is a lifting up and out. It is ingesting through and within. In participation and revelation of beauty and grace, the connection to and generation of Divine energy, consciousness and light is a shared delight.

The Influences from the Stream of Beauty and Grace

The energies, qualities and expanded perspective from the Stream of Beauty and Grace awaken a responsive appreciation of the majesty and elegance that flow in all life. You may be consciously aware that the gifts of each life inspire the gifts of all life. You may feel the reflection of awe, gratitude and celebration as one expression of the Divine flows endlessly in infinite ways to reveal the beauty and grace in all. You may wonder why this is so evident and present for you and so many people miss this artistry in life. Beauty and Grace may inspire you to foster creativity and expression.

How may the Stream of Beauty and Grace influence your life?

Personal Vision inspired by the Stream of Beauty and Grace

You may see the world through inspired revelation that moves you to notice and receive the beauty and grace in life. You may be filled with simple and profound majesty that opens your heart, mind and spirit to the awe and delight of life. You may recognize and appreciate the artistry and the expression of the Divine in all things and in all people. You feel beauty as a revelation and grace as a benediction of being that moves you into greater knowing and appreciation. You are inspired and moved by the beauty you see and the grace you feel in all of life.

Relatedness inspired by the Stream of Beauty and Grace

Beauty and Grace are a spiritual loop of relatedness where beauty shines in inspired awakening and grace gratefully receives the flow of this beauty. In this spiritual loop, grace responds to awaken more beauty and beauty delights in the grace of being. In your relationships, you may be continually present to the beauty of others and moved by their profound inner beauty and soul expression. You may see the hidden treasure of their being and reflect that to them in ways that help them shine. You look at relationships as a dance of emotions, movement, appreciation and love that flow into each other and reflect back in each one's eyes. You appreciate the depth, the creativity and the expression in those you know and are moved to help highlight those miracles and bring them forward.

You seek a way of beauty and grace so that all people can express their gifts, see the beauty in life and support that in creative ways. You understand artful expression as a divine presence and create openings for that revelation to unfold in the lives around you. Reflecting a beloved's beauty to them is a gift you have and share.

World View inspired by the Stream of Beauty and Grace

Beauty and Grace in a world view or cosmic view revels in the flows of creative expression and majesty in all things and in all people. You may seek out ways to support creative expression in the arts and business and life. You encourage visionary, innovative expressions in children and communities as ways for personal communication and as future contributions to growth and harmony. You may help develop trainings and communities that inspire and thrive on innovation as a sustainable creative, circulating flow that contributes to each person and to the world as a whole.

When you think of beauty and grace, when you imagine creating beautiful and elegant solutions, and generous opportunities and collaborations to uplift our world, what does this inspire in you?

Blessings

The Blessings of the Stream of Beauty and Grace

May you perceive and receive the continual
awakening, appreciation, and inspiration
of Beauty and Grace.

May you open to and know an expansion of Divine
recognition, awe and wonder.

May you see, know and feel the living expression,
creativity and revelation of the Divine

May you become a vessel for Divine
revelation and recognition.

CHAPTER ELEVEN:

The Stream of Wisdom

immeasurable knowing penetrates
moments, lifetimes, cosmic cycles and tempos of
time
insight, hindsight, foresight,
flow in rhythms and seas of realization to carry
the knowing

The Stream of Wisdom

The Stream of Wisdom creates a rhythmic knowing of Divine energies and connection. This stream opens the high vibrations of infinite understanding, recognition and presence. It is a weaving of Divine mind, actuality and frequency that invites a direct experience of the Divine with personal and collective expression.

When a person enters and resonates with the Stream of Wisdom, the eternity of the Divine, the connection and revelation of All, becomes whole. The Stream of Wisdom brings a rich and continuing experience of understanding and revelation. Those who have experienced the Stream of Wisdom are infinitely connected. They perceive more of their Divine nature and know Divine connection with each and the All.

The Invitation of the Stream of Wisdom

The Stream of Wisdom is an undulating flow and rhythmic expression of Divine knowing. This flows through a sacred attunement to the All and to the Wisdom in all of its revelations within the All. The Stream of Wisdom is dedicated to the experiencing, supporting, expanding, recovering and holding of wisdom as its spiritual method of attunement and enlightenment. Alignment to Wisdom, as an expression of Divinity, is the highly refined and specific focus of this Stream.

The Stream of Wisdom traces ancient knowing in time and through time. It links and associates each knowing and its related events into a chain of rhythms. This chain of rhythms, of cycles, holds the memory of the ancient. This kind of memory, called deep memory, is an established pattern of connection and interconnection. The rhythm vibrates in a certain frequency which evokes the memory of events, sequences and relationships. As the rhythm pulses and evokes the memory, the ancient knowings are triggered. The Stream of Wisdom moves as a rhythmic, timeless sounding of knowing, evoked by memory, but held in every cycle of existence.

The Invocation of the Stream of Wisdom

The Stream of Wisdom vibrational make-up appears to flow in a longer matrix. The vibrational pattern extends outward and is more durational. Its vibratory patterns move in longer strokes through time. Therefore, one could view the Stream of Wisdom as waves within the great cycle of knowing, reverberating through time and space to illuminate the brilliant interconnections of the Divine.

The vibrational focus of the Stream of Wisdom is rhythmic. The specific patterns collected to create this stream in the very ancient past were a system of rhythms, of cyclic organized motions, that elicit and invoke memory and experience of the whole, even when initially only a portion of the rhythm is revealed.

This is a sequential, cyclical rhythm, that evolves over time with many influences contributing to that rhythm. The Stream of Wisdom may trace back many thousands of years recognizing and appreciating the contributions of different experiences, understandings and illuminations that contribute to a deep knowing. This is not an exclusivity or attachment to a theme. This is the wonder, respect and appreciation of the universal brilliance that flows and can be followed throughout time, to create influence and enlightenment today.

The wisdom of interrelatedness is poetic. Every action does link to another in a direct manner, and influences the interrelatedness and association of all people, known or unknown. The Stream of Wisdom brings people into the understanding that what they do truly affects all of humanity and all consciousness.

As you recognize cyclical rhythms that flow immediately and over time, you can understand and appreciate the long and evolving influence of wisdom. Ancient ways of being contribute to this present moment. Deep understanding of each person and this planet opens the flows of ancient rhythms for modern times. The words may change, the perceptions may adapt, and the wisdom reverberates throughout time and place and beyond. Even though it may appear random or unknown, the poetry of it might suggest that there is no real or pragmatic significance in the interrelatedness and association. The Stream of Wisdom brings people into the understanding that what they do truly affects all of humanity and all consciousness.

The Experience of the Stream of Wisdom

The Stream of Wisdom embraces the connected flow of all wisdom, knowing, stories, vibrational brilliance in rhythmic ribbons of insight. The understanding that what one individual does truly affects all of humanity is gaining momentum. This understanding that what you do in the supermarket can affect someone across the globe is becoming a true perception. This understanding has collected through the Stream of Wisdom. This interrelatedness shows with clarity that your actions directly influence all life everywhere. That interrelatedness, that sequence of events that produces or influences the waves on the beach in Hawaii and the insights you have in one moment are felt and experienced as rhythm. That rhythm can also provide a resonance of wisdom that can be held and accessed.

The rhythms moving within the Stream of Wisdom are recalled in ancient memories. Ancient memories follow the threads of wisdom and experience, through all times and all present moments. They link to moments before time and moments through time to weave the Divine knowing and experience into a rich fullness. These memories are often revealed in stories, legends, songs, dance and the arts. The memories are depicted and brought back into conscious awareness through the memory of the people flowing within the culture that is held within the Stream of Wisdom. The memory, also moving in relationship with the All and the One, flows and connects with what is needed in all of the wisdom, to hook into and retrieve a special vibrational thread of energy that is related to and necessary for the wisdom and revelation at hand. This is a very specific focus of the Stream of Wisdom. Every story, every dance, every memory traces itself to and through the cycles of creation. Every piece of clothing, every piece of art traces itself back to an experience of life or an experience of the cosmic that is held in collective and individual knowing. Every migratory pattern of the birds, turn of the wind, swelling of a bud reveals the nature of the Divine and also displays the relationships which are interconnected at the moment and which will effect change at the time.

These relationships and interrelationships suggest, reveal and teach specific spiritual patterns of energy and knowing that are connections and infusions of Divine energy which inspire, uplift and awaken. The deep memory of an individual or a group working within and influenced by the Stream of Wisdom is dedicated toward spiritual awakening and delight. The thread of focus, the vibrational pattern which holds the energy and attentions for accessing and experiencing spiritual awakening is the focus of Wisdom, of noticing, holding, remembering and keeping the vast conscious interrelated occurrences that influence life and being in your world.

In the flows of spiritual experience, the Stream of Wisdom focuses on holding ancient memory. Following the threads of all known and held relationships, something as small as winds coming off of the plains in spring, the process of dying yarn a particular color of yellow, knowing and remembering the migratory patterns of birds and the turning of constellations - each and every one of these memories signifies the great Divine All. Each and every one of these memories carries deep and experiential wisdom. Memory and wisdom describe states of being and modes of awakening, not simply the storage and retrieval of information.

Within the Stream of Wisdom, memory and wisdom bring awakening. Memory and wisdom activate and accelerate spiritual enlightenment and total communion. When an individual recalls an incident, which is specifically related to this moment in time, they call that knowing into the present moment. In so doing, they activate that energy. This energy, which is revealed in the memory, once again activates the wisdom of the circumstances or event. The memory or wisdom that is recalled, that is brought into the present moment, infuses this present moment with the specific vibrational energies that were (and still are) active in the other piece of wisdom. This is an expanded present, instilled with wisdom spanning time, that contributes to the illumination of this very moment.

Specifically, we are talking about spiritual states of knowing, being and communing. To follow this thread an example of farming is best. A group of individuals are sitting together discussing farming and the season and planting to come. The lands are vast and certain climate conditions prevail, generally speaking. These climate conditions give specific plant life their hardiness and water conditions. Temperatures, soil, fertility of the soil and the weather of the next season all have an influence on the strength and health of the crops to be planted this year.

The group is talking about which crops to plant and which fields to use this season. A light breeze comes up and for a moment everyone enjoys the sweet air. Someone starts to remember this breeze. There is something very familiar about the sweetness of the air and the slight moist quality. Another person, who is also triggered by this same breeze, recalls a story about a breeze like this. Someone, knowing that in their forty-five years planting crops they have never experienced a breeze like this, goes into a state where they are guided to look at an old tapestry that they just know has some clues about the significance of this breeze. As the pieces fall together, individually and collectively they recognize that this breeze signifies a very moist year. The ancient story speaks of it, the tapestry depicts it and the meditation confirms it. It has been dry for quite some time and certain planting fields were selected for their ability to retain moisture in seasons of severe drought.

Knowing that this season is going to have abundant rain and moisture, different fields are selected to be cultivated. Those responsible for the seed selection will do so based on the plant's ability and needs in regards to a wetter season and more rain. Certain nutrients will be added to the soil to take advantage of this season's particular weather. This rain will produce a greater yield, and therefore plans are made to construct storage buildings to house the excess crops. If the crop yield exceeds even this expectation, negotiations with neighbors will be made to help bring in the crop. These considerations and many more, all come into play and organization because the focus of the Stream is Wisdom, this reveals the flow and activation of memory and knowing in the experience and expression of the Divine.

This example shows how many intertwined aspects can be held in one rhythmic event. The breeze unveils a cascade of experiences and knowings, which then reveal specific ways of being or actions to take. This is also the same way spiritual connection is followed and integrated. Spiritual experience flows through the rhythms of wisdom and links all known expressions of spirituality into one multi-leveled expression of the Divine. This multi-leveled expression is available for direct experience. It is held within the focus of the Stream of Wisdom and accessed through the cycles and rhythms of awareness.

Through the Stream of Wisdom, you can receive expansion and awakening to greater levels of insight and spirit. You can also contribute to that endless diversity of knowing and experience. Through the Stream of Wisdom, you can feel fully related to the Divine Source. You will experience the direct memory of this connection and the wisdom of this connection in a full and palpable way. You form a profound connection by being able to feel the flows of wisdom and memory. You can also form a strong energy and recognition of contribution.

This energy of connection, of receiving the blessings and generosity of the flows of wisdom and ancient knowing, pulses through the Stream of Wisdom. An individual experiencing this connection contributes to the stream's collective nature. The individual's experience contributes to the Stream of Wisdom without altering the energy of the stream. It is as though the Stream of Wisdom seems to take into consideration a new way of receiving or participating with the key patterns of Wisdom, and they become notated. In this way, an individual is reciprocal in being able to go beyond the childlike notion of only receiving energy, but also recognizing the capacity to contribute, to give to the great flow that supports all life.

Participating with the Stream of Wisdom, you can move in rhythmic expression of Divine knowing. The cycle and pulse of this energy brings new avenues for spiritual awareness and awakening. It brings ancient wisdom through time and contributes to contemporary thought. The Stream of Wisdom holds the ancient and the future in multi-dimensional collaboration within the infinite. It vibrates into an expression of the Divine that conveys continuity. The Stream of Wisdom spans the ages and illuminates the cycles. When cycles are illuminated, they are rhythms. They can be followed and emulated. Knowing the rhythm, you can learn to participate within and create that rhythm. Therein lies the sacred and the access to the Divine.

The Influences from the Stream of Wisdom

The energies, qualities and expanded perspective from the Stream of Wisdom travel through a focus of knowing to bring understanding, truths and revelation into all life. This expression of understanding, experience, divine revelation and perception opens you to the endless presence of knowing. You may feel drawn to the ancient systems and teachings that still hold true for thousands of years. You may see the brilliance of elders and be honored to be in their presence and receive their wisdom. You can feel the pulsing ancient knowing and new awakenings and multi-dimensional brilliance and you are ready to open to more.

How may the Stream of Wisdom influence your life?

Personal Vision inspired by the Stream of Wisdom

Wisdom, the expression of sacred teachings, the experiences of the Divine in all life, inspires you. You may see life as the brilliant expression of the Divine in all things and all beings. You may feel the flow of the ancient sages calling you to remember and create anew. You value wisdom and knowledge and you love learning and experiencing in meaningful and transformational themes that expand your vision and open your heart. You delight in ancient wisdom and contemporary revelations. You are thrilled with pursuit of knowing and to perceive meaning and truth. Your delight in wisdom may inspire you to explore the essence of Divine consciousness, teachings of the ancients, new innovations in technology that change lives, creative and sustainable solutions that empower communities, discoveries in health and wellness, and ways of being that uplift our world. Wisdom reveals itself in many realms.

Relatedness inspired by the Stream of Wisdom
Relatedness is an aspect of wisdom. Everything is related and the sacred wisdom and teachings reveal this in many ways. In personal relationships you value the wisdom of each person and system. You may be a clear space of listening to receive this person's wisdom and to understand the depths of it. You want to know what a person knows and to understand the depths of their perceptions as a contribution and an honoring of their being. Interpersonally, you want to know why and to understand it and receive the wealth of it. With individuals and in community, you want to perceive what is happening and the journey to now. Then cherish that knowledge and experience and if appropriate preserve it as a way of honoring and sharing the depths of being.

You seek a way of wisdom so that all can appreciate the lengths it takes, the dedication it requires and the accomplishment it is to produce, cherish and receive wisdom. You understand and appreciate the life journey each person takes and how it influences their life. You recognize the wisdom in their journey, reflecting that acknowledgement back to them.

World View inspired by the Stream of Wisdom
Wisdom in a world view or cosmic view embraces the collective wisdom from all people, all cultures and all systems. You may seek out collaborations with different people whose wisdom can contribute to helping change systems and situations. You

may travel to different areas to absorb the knowledge and ways of being that bring greater understanding to yourself that you may share this with others. You may initiate teams and groups with a focus of gaining wisdom, knowledge, specialties and applications that will help individuals and communities to thrive. As a wisdom seeker and wisdom communicator you celebrate the meaning, power, interrelatedness and awakening that sharing wisdom can bring to your world.

When you think of wisdom, when you imagine bringing understanding, knowledge, experience and elegant solutions, and conscious opportunities and collaborations to uplift your world, what does this inspire in you?

Blessings

The Blessings of the Stream of Wisdom

May you experience infinite understanding,
recognition and presence that lights your life.

May you live filled with the knowing interrelatedness
and association with all of humanity
and all consciousness

May you receive and know the blessings
from the Divine, humanity and all consciousness
that bring light to shine and wisdom to share.

May you become a vessel for Divine sanctity and
timelessness.

CHAPTER TWELVE:

The Stream of Truth

it is so, in endless verity
of the All and the One
clouds part to reveal the luminous quintessence of
being
clear, whole, reverent, resonance rings true

The Stream of Truth

The Stream of Truth is a vibrating brilliance of Divine clarity, light and frequency that reveals a direct, genuine experience and recognition of the Divine in all things. This awakens pure knowing. This stream reveals and illuminates a clear, authentic experience of Divine truth, transparency and omnipresence.

When a person enters and resonates with the Stream of Truth, the reality of this Divine connection and all experience, becomes whole. The Stream of Truth brings an immediate clarity and understanding of the pristine core of the Divine in the All. Those who have experienced the Stream of Truth are awakening, candid, joyful, open and sincere. They perceive, respect and appreciate the rich clarity of the Divine resonance of the All and the One.

The Invitation of the Stream of Truth

The Stream of Truth is a brilliant light. Truth, in itself, is clarity. It is the utmost clarity of any situation, process, experience or knowing. Truth is the basic, primary experience or knowledge of something or someone. Truth feels like standing on the top of the mountain, surrounded by blue skies and endless views in all directions. It is a level of perception. Knowing the truth is knowing the highest or clearest or most absolute essence.

Truth is a pinnacle experience, a singular expression and an absolute. It is ultimate clarity. It is the fundamental, original and primary occurrence. It is a peak expression, the highest or deepest quality or perception. Knowing, discovering and searching for Truth gives an individual the barometer against which all other experiences can be discerned. By knowing and experiencing truth, all other experiences can be understood within that context. By knowing truth, one can see the relationships of other things or experiences or systems and thereby have a deeper understanding of it all. One can be in the presence of truth and be guided by truth and in this, have deeper experiences in life.

The pristine nature of Truth varies, only in so far as one can know the levels of truth in each situation, circumstance and stage of existence. Often times, truth is revealed. The veils of confusion are lifted in layers and deeper meaning or greater clarity becomes apparent. Truth lies within truth and clarity brings its revelation.

The Invocation of the Stream of Truth

The Stream of Truth vibrates to advanced frequencies that illuminate, awaken and reveal authentic, actual Divine Perfection. Truth is a clear resonance. The frequencies of the Stream of Truth can be as a clearing to reveal the most brilliant. The frequencies of the Stream of Truth can be as a lifting, a raising of perception to experience the originating flow. The frequencies of the Stream of Truth can be as an awakening that 'sees,' knows and resonates with clear perception.

The Stream of Truth is the quest or the focus to discover, explore, hold and resonate to the highest levels of truth that an individual, culture and material form can recognize. This one aspect is specifically illuminating

Vibrationally, truth resonates within many aspects and therefore requires a multi-leveled appreciation. The original understanding of the essence of truth is a clear, impeccable tone of resonance. The truths of existence reveal the miracles of expression. As one stretches to know and experience these truths, they reveal themselves as levels of clarity. They are functional and perceptible truths. These truths may be experienced as deep knowings or scientific discoveries, but perceptionally, there is a core of unshakable purity or fundamentality about them. As the Stream of Truth resonates, it appears louder. Its vibration supersedes other vibrations, and therefore it can become a guiding force. This is why there is a notion of a quest for truth, because the vibration is so genuine and distinct that one will search to find it.

The vibrational construction of the Stream of Truth has two distinct energies to it. Initially, there is a quality of pausing, of experiencing a void, an emptiness. Specifically, the stream is not empty, it is organizing. In the realm of all truths, the Stream of Truth is organizing around the truths you seek or the truths you hold. This aspect of the vibrational energy can feel like touching the void or it can feel like a clear and moving emptiness.

The second energy of the Stream of Truth is the sounding. It is like the clear ringing of a large bell. Once the energy of truth is organized and collected, the resonance is known and it appears. The clarity of this truth, this vibrational wholeness is profound. It can feel like the clearest light or the brightest sound. As the initial collecting forces of organization feel more like a pause in energy than anything specific, the impact of the second energy resonance of truth feels strong and vibrant and whole. It is as though its presence announces itself. This is why you may feel something 'rings true.'

There is a very distinct vibrational wholeness to the resonance of truth. The description of the vibrational make-up of the Stream of Truth as two distinct energies or waves of the same essence is provided to simplify locating or experiencing this Stream of Consciousness. This double oscillation is very immediate and may not even be noticed, especially since the emptiness of organization is so brief and the ringing of truth is infinitely durational. In many respects, the effects of the stream are more observable than the stream itself. Just as hitting one note on a stringed instrument will make all the other stringed instruments in that room vibrate to that same note. So too, the Stream of Truth can cause all individuals experiencing the truth to resonate to that truth.

The Experience of the Stream of Truth

In the search to experience a greater level of divinity, of inner purpose and connectedness in life, truth is a barometer. As a measure, truth can guide you to higher and more profound experiences of consciousness and being. The Stream of Truth is the resonance of this energy, clearing the way for the vitality of the Divine to reveal itself.

The Stream of Truth is the resonance of truth. This clarity provides a guidance system wherein an individual can always feel the kinship with truth, clarity, primary or fundamental energies and move toward them for a direct experience. Resonating in harmony with the absolute is key to understanding the nature of life. It is key to holding the highest integrity of being, not merely as a quality or what may be considered a morality. You hold the highest integrity of truth, because it is a clear and objective wholeness. The resonance of truth is an unadulterated experience of life, the Divine and the genuine expression of the highest levels of being. It may appear to be ethical, moral or good, or have a particular judgment or value, but the primary reason for the alignment is in its own clarity of experience. In this pure wisdom, in the direct experience of truth, the view is endless and yet very distinct. Any embellishment, any alteration in the resonance of truth is a distraction.

Vibrationally, the Stream of Truth moves to reveal the essence of truth. This stream is resonating to truth in each and every experience. It desires to find the truth of any experience of knowing. It seeks perfect pitch in any arena.and all areas. There are several different aspects of truth that can be discovered and used as guides.

TRUTH AS PRIMARY. The Truth can be viewed or experienced as something fundamental or primary. Understanding the element of light or sound is understanding a fundamental, a truth. This avenue of seeking truth reveals the primary nature of the issue. This primary or fundamental nature of truth can be the most basic denominator or the smallest part that can be known and still contain the essence of itself or its core expression.

TRUTH AS CLARITY. The Truth can be revealed as clear or unpolluted. This aspect of truth would reveal the complete essence that is unembellished or diminished. It would be 24 karat gold. Nothing has been added to it. Nothing has been subtracted from it. The essence of it is whole and unadulterated and it shines on its own.

TRUTH AS DISTINCTION. Another way the Truth is revealed is by recognizing distinction. The truth is separate and distinguished from other things, notions and events. It is its own definition, its own genuine self. It separates itself from other knowings or experiences. It is true and authentic, which distinguishes itself from all other aspects and experiences which do not hold this resonance.

TRUTH AS ABSOLUTE. Truth can also be known and revealed through its absolute nature. It is the genuine expression. It is the actuality of itself. True north is the absolute direction of north. It is whole, in and of itself. It is complete and genuine. If a person is perceiving true north, they are locked into the absolute resonance of it. The needle on the compass is unwavering. If a person is experiencing true clarity, they are held within the resonance of the most enlightened knowing.

Since Truth can be known or experienced or perceived as primary or clear or distinct or absolute, the Stream of Truth becomes somewhat more richly complex as a life guidance system. Truth can be known and experienced within any quality. You can find the true nature of anything or any experience. You can look for the true meaning of life, the true career to pursue, the true property of physical matter, the true story of political intrigue. There is truth to be found in everything. There is a true nature of many things. There are many absolutes. There are many primary expressions and colors. While some may search for only one truth, the resonance of truth itself is a very rich expression of the Divine. This applies to the Stream of Truth.

The resonance of truth can also be found in every other resonance. As truth is the pristine wholeness of an experience or essence, then the most clear or fundamental energy of any particular quality is known as its true nature. Musically, perfect pitch is the clearest resonance of the musical notes. One who has perfect pitch can sing every note with the utmost clarity. The sound does not waver. The vibration does not diminish or expand. The singer sings the precise note. If the singer is singing the note A, then they are singing the exact and full vibration of that note. Playing any instrument tuned to that note will reveal an exact pitch. All of those instruments, including the singer, will strike a perfect sounding and vibration of that note. It is unwavering and exact. One who can hear in perfect pitch can hear the slightest variation from the perfect vibration of each note. If the singer or any of the instruments were off key, off pitch, this person would hear it very distinctly. They would hear the variation so distinctly that it would be painful and obvious. The true pitch becomes obvious. The truth of the musical note can be experienced by singing one note. It can also be experienced by listening to all the notes. Each note has its true vibration and all notes have their true vibration. In essence, you can know the truth from one perspective or from the benefit of many perspectives. The truth, in itself, still rings clear.

To know something of truth is to know or have a primary understanding, to touch the fundamental or core of a subject. It is the depth or even singularity of a system. When you speak of "true love," you are referring to the deepest understanding and knowing of love. By using the term "true love" you are also saying that all other loves were not as clear, not as fundamental, not as singular in their purpose or essence. Truth is a primary knowing and against this knowing, other ideas or experiences seem embellished. They are encumbered by something else or unnecessarily adorned.

The experience of truth reveals an energy that stands alone in vision. Often truth is a quest unto itself. As the focus of a quest - "the quest for truth," then truth becomes the object which is sought. Truth becomes a goal, an aspiration, an indicator of the heights of knowing or spiritual light. The quest for truth is the search for the clearest meaning or experience. You search for the pure wisdom. You search for the absolute truth, the primary experience. The quest for truth becomes the search for the ultimate knowing or experience, whether you search for true love, true wisdom or the true nature of life.

The Influences from the Stream of Truth

The energies, qualities and resonant perspective from the Stream of Truth brings clear, unembellished knowing and perception. This elegant pristine knowing resonates to higher levels of awakening and expression and is a singular sensation of direct divine essence. You may pursue truth as the beacon from which all experience may flow in your life. You may appreciate the deep meaning and transformational effects that truth reveals and bestows. You can feel the absolute essence of truth and this tends to be a pinnacle expression and pursuit in all things for you. Truth guides you.

How may the Stream of Truth influence your life?

Personal Vision inspired by the Stream of Truth

Truth is a brilliance that lights your way and helps you see clearly into your own soul's being and into the souls of others. You may see the world in relative relationships of truth, while you seek to know the core of it. You may be discerning and penetrating in your pursuit and delight in truth. You may favor stripping away the embellishments to see, know and grasp the authentic heart of clear perception. You are excited by revelations of deeper knowing, transparent understanding, unshakable purity and genuine relatedness. You may be a truth seeker.

Relatedness inspired by the Stream of Truth

Truth is a fundamental of relatedness. Relationships, community, connections and interpersonal associations thrive and expand with honesty and truth. In recognition of a state of being and an individual's or group's spoken or unspoken truth, relatedness, honor, appreciation and respect flow to create depths and genuine connection. You may appreciate people speaking truth to you, sharing their real feelings, opening their opinions so you may see and know them in authenticity. You may speak from the heart, with your highest integrity and clarity to relay true communication as it is. You celebrate and appreciate people who will speak and live without guile. You see truth in others as their deeper meaning and purpose, revealed in who they are, what they do and how they live in the world.

You seek a way of truth so that all people can have the clarity to make decisions and feel the resonance of their being in the highest light. You experience truth as a way and guidance system for bringing out the highest, the more effective and the greatest in each person. You delight in seeing, awakening and celebrating the truth in each person's life and being.

World View inspired by the Stream of Truth

Truth in a world view or cosmic view is a clearing place where distinctions for the higher good and the greater experience in all people is revealed. Revealing and distinguishing truth makes greater strides for individuals and community that generate accessible, attainable and actionable guidelines for living. You may seek out ways to bring truth, to bring fundamental understanding into communities that creates an interrelatedness based on genuine knowing and caring. You may teach or guide individuals to higher learning and communication so they may become righteous leaders in their own communities, also teaching from truth. As a truth seeker you shine a light to reveal the genuine, the real and the resonant highest truth so each and all can follow that beacon to make beneficial contributions in the world.

When you think of truth, when you imagine unveiling a deeper knowledge, genuine expression and clear solutions, opportunities and collaborations to uplift our world, what does this inspire in you?

Blessings

The Blessings of the Stream of Truth

May you presence truth as a very clear, rich,
vibrating enlightening expression of the Divine.

May you know highest integrity of being,
as a pristine and objective wholeness and
recognition of the Divine.

May you celebrate and know the beauty within the
clarity and essence of life.

May you become a vessel for Divine clarity,
illumination and recognition.

CHAPTER THIRTEEN:

The Stream of Radiance

shining forces illuminating perception
transmit beauty, adoration, awakening into the
absolute never-ending light
revelations, resonate reverberating the blessings
gifts of being in Divine recognition

The Stream of Radiance

The Stream of Radiance is an illuminating Divine brilliance
that reveals a clarity, light, frequency and recognition of the
Divine flow. This accelerates and illuminates a clear, awakening
experience of Divine truth, enlightenment and beauty.

When a person enters and resonates with the Stream of
Radiance, the reality of this Divine light becomes experiential.
The Stream of Radiance brings an immediate and growing
embrace of the Divine as personal and Universal. Those who
have experienced the Stream of Radiance are shining, clear,
joyful, loving and focused. They perceive and share the true
brilliance of the Divine in All.

The Invitation of the Stream of Radiance

The Stream of Radiance pulses upliftment. This resonating, radiating, stream conducts and influences higher vibratory frequencies of Divine blessing and generosity. It holds and releases endless supplies of light and joy. Frequencies shift and become a shining forth to transmit wisdom, knowing, illumination and connectivity.

Within the energies of this Stream, the new and vibrant illuminate the ancient and deep. The wisdom of the past, of the centuries of knowledge and spirituality are illuminated by new energies and pathways. This combining fusion enhances the vibratory patterns of the ancestral knowledge, rites and deep earth wisdoms with the new light that is traveling to the planet and toward human consciousness. It combines both aspects of expanded awakening and brings them together in a view of wholeness and appreciation. The ancient ways and understandings are embraced as they enrich the most recent discovery. The newer ideas and practices are celebrated as untried phenomena that augments the oldest wisdom. They radiate separately and together. Each aspect of light, from the beginning of its journey to its newest contacts is savored and explored. This is following the Stream of Radiance.

This endless circulation of light continually emits vibrational patterns that generate awakening and spiritual advancement. Light is a specific vibration. Those vibrating energies create light and colors of light due to certain patterns and resonances. Light also travels. It moves from its source of resonance outward. It moves from its origin, the place emitting the frequencies of light, outward as far as it can go, based on the intensity of the light and the obstacles in its path. This is Radiance. Radiance is the brilliance of energy and its traveling factors. To be radiant, as light is radiant, a substance has to emit energy beyond its containment field.

The Invocation of the Stream of Radiance

The Stream of Radiance transmits Divine energy outward from the center of the Universe, from the core of being and towards this planet, specifically to those people who are in line to receive this energy. Radiance is the property of how something is moved. It is the procedure of energy and light from somewhere to somewhere. This motion, this directed energy, feels a particular way simply because it is directed, it is transmitting something from somewhere to somewhere. That which is sent, the light, the frequencies, the transformational energy, emanates from the core, from the Divine focus, and flows toward and to earth and the specific individuals in line with that flow.

Radiance is the capacity and energy of sending from the center outward. It is vivid, glowing or shining light or energy that is transmitted. This is the quality and property of the Stream of Radiance. The Stream emits Divine energy by radiating it and certain experiences unfold because an individual feels the radiance of the stream. The motion of traveling, of emitting high frequency Divine blessing in directed motion, is part of the influence of the Stream of Radiance.

The Experience of the Stream of Radiance

The qualities of the resonance of the Stream of Radiance are for upliftment. Therefore, the vibrations that are coming from the Stream of Radiance will create a pattern that moves an individual to a relatively higher experience or perspective. The individual can interpret that experience in many ways, but it is the properties of radiance that bring about this new perspective. The patterns of vibration and resonance send energy forward that generates a new perspective. This perspective is a combination or blending of ancient wisdoms which may already be known with new wisdom which may yet have been perceived. The blending of both resonates and radiates an individual to a new understanding. This is an expansion.

An expansion takes place when an individual receives the energies of radiance. They are transformed by the energy emitted from the stream and therefore open to encompass a greater capacity for light and for receiving light. This opening is an expansion to accommodate the increase in light and energy.

The Stream of Radiance elicits awakening and conscious presence. Spiritual vision becomes more clear and spiritual connection becomes more pronounced. This energy is sent out toward anyone who wishes to partake of this incandescence. It radiates, sends out, emits a shining force. When you are held within the Stream of Radiance, you are participating with the radiance and can also become a source of light. You can resonate to the energies of the Stream of Radiance and become a radiating factor of this light and uplifting spiritual energy.

The vibrational patterns of the Stream of Radiance are varied. While there are unifying factors that distinguish this stream from the others, part of that distinction is the changing frequencies that modulate the emissions of light. The light which is radiated is relatively constant, but the ways that the light is radiated and the ways that it travels vary depending on the circumstance. They differ, modify and alternate in resonance, frequency, reach and duration.

A remarkable aspect of the Stream of Radiance is that resonating within the Stream you can become very aware that there is no such thing as spiritual energy. There is no demarcation between what is spiritual and what is mundane. Participating within the Stream of Radiance you can see that all is spiritual energy. Every particle of being and existence can be and is a source of illumination. Every plane of existence is a place of enlightenment. The Stream of Radiance reveals that the Divine shines through every aspect of being and nothing is exempt from that brilliance. By experiencing the emanations of the Stream of Radiance you begin to resonate with that essence. By resonating to the forces which radiate upliftment and great clarity, you begin to generate a level of radiance. Once a person or being is radiating at a particular level, then it is exceedingly obvious that this brilliance was always present and available.

The Stream of Radiance enhances life by radiating advanced levels of Divine energy which produce upliftment, community and an encompassing level of appreciation for the totality of existence. By resonating with the ancient wisdom and illuminating it, while at the same time highlighting the most recent wisdom and illuminating it, the Stream of Radiance brings expanding awakening.

What is being sent from the Stream of Radiance can also be experienced similar to the emotions and qualities as love, confidence and joy. It appears as though the quality of love is present in the Stream of Radiance, but it is a by-product of the emanating essence of the stream. When you feel the pure incandescence of a radiance of clear light, you can easily feel it as love, unconditional and unrestrained love. When you feel the flows of light transmitted from the Stream of Radiance it can feel like joy and delight. You can feel uplifted and enmeshed in the exuberance of all creation. The specific qualities and frequency patterns of joy have not been transmitted, but you can feel joy through the energies, associations and transformational flows of the Stream of Radiance.

This radiance is transformational and transferable. Joy is a radiant quality. Joy, as an emotion, is experienced as a particular property or feeling and at the same time it radiates from the individual feeling it. Joy moves outward from its source in the individual experiencing joy, outward into the world. If this joyful individual is in a crowd of people, then those people will be touched by the joy emanating from this individual. If this individual is talking on the phone, then joy will be transmitted through the phone call. If this individual is walking down the street, then the joy will radiate outward from this individual to all of those in a line with the flow of joy. The influence of the Stream Of Radiance expands and this accelerates the frequencies.

The word, acceleration, in a spiritual sense means to advance in speed and vibration. An individual's personal vibration, their emanations of life essence and consciousness, advances and resonates faster. This allows perception to become clearer and more refined. Clarity and refinement in your own perceptions provide a greater experience of awakening.

As the Stream of Radiance is one of radiance and is not related to a specific quality unto itself, then you can experience the clarity of radiance and gain access to the changes in velocity and what influence they have on spiritual or consciousness advancement. You could feel the glowing nature of the stream and feel what it is to glow. You could feel the brilliance of that energy and resonate to that particular perspective of clarity. An individual could connect with the shining nature of this energy and stream and experience the celebration that it generates. He could feel that resonance traveling outward from Divine Source, from the central core of consciousness and influencing all that it encounters. Another individual may feel joy, may feel unconditional love, may revel in the celebration of all being, because they are part of the radiant energies of the Divine. The Stream of Radiance doesn't impart that translation of emotions, it simply carries that exultation and the individual experiences it. The brilliance of Stream of Radiance is that once you encounter that traveling and accelerating energy of the Divine, you can become a part of the radiance of the Divine All.

The Influences from the Stream of Radiance

The energies, qualities and expanded vibrations from the Stream of Radiance illuminates and resonates to shine the highest clear, joyful, loving and focused brilliance into your world and all beings therein. This clear expression transmits Divine revelation in concordance with blessing, generosity and connectivity. You may expand your being to receive the radiance of awakening and revelation for personal transformation and enlightenment. You may celebrate this shining forth to experience multiple and continuous Divine connection. You can feel the presence of the Divine in all aspects of life and being.

How may the Stream of Radiance influence your life?

Personal Vision inspired by the Stream of Radiance

Radiance is a shining and a recognition of the Divine and awakens the brilliance in you and others. The radiance within oneself, and the radiance in the All ignites a clear recognition, perception, understanding and appreciation of the immediate, eternal all-pervasive presence of the Divine. You may feel the energy of light igniting inspiration, creativity, recognition and appreciation throughout your being. You may be filled with delight and wonder and joy and spirit that moves you to share your gifts. You are shining and that true vibration lights your own being and lights your way.

Relatedness inspired by the Stream of Radiance

Relatedness inspired by the Stream of Radiance celebrates the light in people, beings, places and consciousness. Relationships inspired by radiance encourage each person and each community to shine. In relationship with others, you may encourage them to shine, to step beyond their cloistered nature and share their brilliance. You may see and recognize another's radiance and reflect their beauty to them in ways that they can see your respect, appreciation and joy for their gifts. You may be comfortable to step back and let another shine so they can discover and experience their radiance. You may appreciate those who recognize brilliance in others and share the brilliance of others in a truly blessing way. You feel and know another's blessings and within your personal relationships and community you seek to help others shine and bring their gifts, talents and perspective forward as a gift.

You seek a way of radiance so that all people can share with joy, wisdom and appreciation. You know and experience the goodness, the beauty and the sanctity of each person as a truth that shines forward. You are moved by revealing the radiance of one and all and the whole planet as a pure and rich radiance of the Divine All.

World View inspired by the Stream of Radiance

Radiance in a world view or cosmic view reveals innumerable ways to celebrate the gifts of others and shine light into the world. Perceiving life as a resonating focus, you seek out those who graciously shine and celebrate their beauty and wisdom. You also may seek out those who are unaware of their shining forth to encourage them to light the way for themselves and others. You may teach or guide individuals in many disciplines to create pathways and systems that bring greater truth, connection, relatedness and opportunities for growth and beauty. You may focus on shining a light on aspects that need direction and resolution. You may also focus attention on circumstances that are illuminating the world and attracting consciousness for focus on that illumination to gain momentum, healing and sacred community.

When you think of radiance, when you imagine shining a light on true knowledge, brilliant people and transformational solutions, opportunities and collaborations to uplift our world, what does this inspire in you?

Blessings

The Blessings of the Stream of Radiance

May you be a shining force for clear, joyful, loving
beauty from Divine Source.

May you transmit glowing knowing
illumination in this world.

May the radiance of the Divine All
fill your life in celebration of community,
wisdom and unconditional love.

May you become a joyful vessel for Divine light.

CHAPTER FOURTEEN:

The Stream of Reciprocity

the endless flow nurtures communal unity
interconnected relatedness linked in circuits of light
an interchange feeds one and all
continually together in sacred dance

The Stream of Reciprocity

The Stream of Reciprocity is a flowing interconnected Divine
matrix that reveals a related influence and response of the
Cosmic All. This distinguishes a clear experience of Divine
presence and communion.

When a person enters and resonates with the Stream of
Reciprocity, the reality of the interconnection of All, becomes
a powerful awakening. The Stream of Reciprocity brings an
immediate and growing recognition of the relationships and
connections of personal, Universal and Divine exchange. Those
who have experienced the Stream of Reciprocity are inspired,
aware, caring, influential and generous. They understand and
live the interrelatedness of the Divine in All.

The Invitation of the Stream of Reciprocity

The Stream of Reciprocity illuminates the recognition of the mutual exchange of all energies and things. It illustrates a deep understanding that everything responds and corresponds to everything else, somewhere and somehow. The results of the effects may be unknown or obscure, but there are effects. That is certain. Everything has a response to something else. Everything corresponds to something else. Everything has an influence upon something else and everything is influenced by something else. Nothing is alone and separate in the world or in the Cosmic All.

There is a deep and resonating fact within this that binds all people, all situations together. If there is a mutual exchange of energies in the world, in the universe, then what unfolds in one place has a direct influence on what unfolds in another. If what happens in one place effects what happens in another place, then one is influenced by matters that may not be of initial concern but can be important later. As the world gets smaller and smaller, this is evident and even obvious. In ancient times, it was less pronounced and therefore the illumination of this wisdom creates a profound effect on life and living, today.

Recognition of the mutual exchange of influences reveals that the rains of this season will affect the crops of the next. The use of one product will necessitate its replenishment, so it may be used again. In planting and agriculture, one can see that the influences of seasonal weather patterns would be watched, charted and understood because the rhythms of the weather have a direct influence on an individual's life. One's family's and community's existence depend upon the appropriate arrival of rains and sun. This rain and sunshine feeds the crops, which feed the family and the animals. This understanding of reciprocity is an understanding of how life feeds and nourishes itself. It reveals how life influences itself and either sustains, balances or destroys itself. The Stream of Reciprocity can be seen as the causation of the world.

The Stream of Reciprocity is profound and is used as a guiding force of knowing and spiritual truth. Posed as a question, if everything is reciprocal, if everything has an influence on something else, then does one action or one series of actions have an influence on everything? Does one good crop change life for generations of progeny? Does one bad crop alter existence for a whole community?

Under the influence of the Stream of Reciprocity, the answer to the above questions is yes. Everything that occurs has an influence on something else. The universe moves in response to a mutual give and take. Life mutually responds to life. What happens in one place can influence what happens in another. The more one is aware of this reciprocity, the more influence one has and the more adequately one can respond to life in all of its revelations.

The Invocation of the Stream of Reciprocity

Vibrationally, the Stream of Reciprocity extends a compatible flow of resonance to all other areas of consciousness. Within this stream each aspect of being has a frequency signature and relatedness. Each nuance of energy, each understanding, wisdom and action creates a vibrational pattern and thread that is sympathetically released and shared. The vibrations extended express the overall mutual relationship and influence of the universe. As part of the Streams of Consciousness traveling to this planet, they express the interrelated mutual influence that circumstances on this planet have with each other and with the Universal All. The vibrational patterns are aligned so that one can feel and know how the flows of energy can and do influence all of life.

The vibrational context of the Stream of Reciprocity shows the beauty and elegance of mutually corresponding events. It reveals a companionship and complementary force of being within the Universal All. Through understanding and discovering this companionship, an individual can experience a great inner knowing of place in the All. The interwoven nature, the influential sphere of every action and event does indeed reveal the importance of each individual in the scheme of reality in all worlds and all times. The Stream of Reciprocity reveals that the mutual interchange of energies is certain. Everything in the universe is an exchange of mutual influences. Bringing this to a more expansive view, the actions a person takes influences how the universe reveals itself.

Each vibrational pattern and thread in the Stream of Reciprocity is sympathetically released and shared with all other vibrations that can accommodate that energy. Furthermore, even those vibrations and patterns that cannot specifically accommodate that energy or that wisdom are influenced by the vibrations shared universally. This influence may be direct or indirect, depending on the mutual relatedness of the receiving energy or its proximity and compatibility. The Stream of Reciprocity sends energy out to those vibrations and systems that can respond to it. Those that can respond are mutually compatible and their influences are shared. Those that are beyond direct influence or are not mutually beneficial to the experience may be influenced, but not directly. This provides the growth and opportunity for greater knowing. In this energy exchange, the Stream of Reciprocity also receives vibrations, wisdom and information that it then processes and imparts.

The Experience of the Stream of Reciprocity

The actions one takes influence one's individual life and all life. The thoughts one generates influences one's individual life and all life. Each and every thing influences each and every thing. This brilliance of interrelatedness, concurrence, responsiveness, synergy, interconnection and participation all flow with the Stream of Reciprocity. You can have a greater knowing of personal influence and personal relatedness. One aspect is the full truth that 'you are not alone,' not only in the knowing of spiritual and Divine connection, but in the truth of personal influence and relatedness. Each individual matters, is important and influences all. This can be seen and felt. The beauty and vibrational alignment of the Stream of Reciprocity reveals that one being does make a difference and the choice of that difference influences a corresponding flow. Even reading this right now, feeling the wisdom, aligning with your thoughts and participation in life, reveals the Stream of Reciprocity in your life and the many ways you may consciously express the mutual exchange of your wisdom, action and blessing.

Actions and the responses to action become a way of moving in the world. As the Stream of Reciprocity expands, it can appear that if an individual knows the influences and results of the stream, they can change the qualities and experiences in their life. This can and will influence the world and the Cosmic All.

You could interpret this same understanding that thoughts, actions, ideas and words send out an energy that has a reciprocal response in the universe. The response possesses the same general qualities and moves outward from the originating source and also in reciprocal motion toward the source from which the originating energy was sent. The vibrational pattern of the Stream of Reciprocity resonates to this energy and beyond it. Humanity and life add something to the response. An individual's reaction may be amplified, altered, decreased, transformed, and unexpected thusly expanding, contacting or modifying the energy. An individual's reaction may not occur as immediate and may build or decrease over time. When you understand that thoughts, actions, ideas and words send out an energy which generates a response in the universe, you have the opportunity to consciously contribute more blessings in your world.

The Stream of Reciprocity could be seen as that whatever a person does, they will in some way experience the effects of those actions. It is not simply the outward actions or deeds that generate a response. Ideas, thoughts, emotions and conversations are included as well. The simplest way to understand this collective reach is that anything that will cause a ripple of energy in the Cosmic All has a response that is generated by it. A thought can cause a ripple in the Cosmic All. An intention can cause a ripple in the Cosmic All. A thought may not cause as big of a ripple as a deed. Of course, some thoughts actually cause bigger ripples than deeds, because the thought generated greater deeds than would have unfolded without the thought.

Imagine that an individual feels joy, which stems from someone giving them a sum of money that will help them pay for their needs for quite some time. This person is very pleased and begins sharing their good fortune with others. This sharing of good fortune exceeds the amount of money, for this individual is also sharing their gratitude and love and appreciation for receiving this unexpected gift. The reaction to the gift is greater than the gift itself. The financial gift, which will help this individual's family live healthy lives and contribute to the community in unforeseen ways, is expanded by the recipient's elation and sharing of good fortune. The energy of reciprocity is expanded beyond the gift. This happens because of human reaction, not by natural laws of physics.

The notion that there is a relationship between your actions and the universe, is in direct relationship with the Stream of Reciprocity. Yet how this influences and benefits is always in motion. The universe responds, based on the response and sensitivity of those experiencing the motion. So, in the above example, the sum of money generated more good will than is normal for that sum or for that amount of generosity. There are long reaching effects from this generosity. The joy generated by receiving the sum of money is directly created and spread by the recipient, but all of this joy and gratitude is inspired by the donor, the person who gave the gift. Who has incurred the focus of the reciprocity? All benefit. Each person, each system, each reverberation receives the expanding influence of this generosity. The Stream of Reciprocity expands the considerations and spheres of influence of actions, thoughts and their corresponding reverberations.

Experienced through the Stream of Reciprocity, there is a sharing in the vibrational sense of reciprocity. It is inclusive. Everyone will eventually be influenced by the energy and vibration because nothing is separate in the Cosmic All. Understanding the levels and nuances of reciprocity can reach into every aspect of life. It can influence the pragmatic actions an individual takes and the philosophical path an individual pursues. The vibrational energies of the Stream of Reciprocity shows that everything is influenced by something else. If that is extended, everything is influenced by everything else sooner or later. This is the nature of cycles. Cycles are the rhythms of life that influence each other. A cycle can be quick, meaning a cycle of one day. A cycle can be long as in the revolution of a galaxy. Each cycle has a direct influence on life based on what it encounters and expresses. The fullness of the concurrent relationships within any cycle is miraculous. The amount of mutually corresponding events unfolding in one moment are pragmatically incalculable. The mutual dependence that flows from every corner of creation to every corner of creation is brilliant and breathtaking.

How humans respond to the energies of a Stream of Consciousness creates new choices and ideas. The responses and choices are translations of reality and become models of experience. The quality of energy from the individual Stream of Consciousness doesn't necessarily change. The quality of the inspired stream may not change, but it may indeed encompass another view, another interpretation. This helps those participating with the stream to grow and expand in consciousness.

Understanding and working with respect to mutual recognition, the flows of energy that highlight the Stream of Reciprocity can encourage a new view of living. It can herald a deeper understanding and appreciation of all life. It is not the purpose of this discussion to discover or suggest ways of compensating for past losses. It is to disclose how the flows of energy influence people and cultures and civilizations.

By knowing and recognizing the Streams of Consciousness you can understand how certain people, cultures and civilizations grow and relate. In that level understanding, healing, renewal and appreciation can supplant confusion and resentment. A new recognition and understanding can add to new levels of mutual relatedness. The flows of reciprocity can expand a new sense of relatedness and appreciation.

Recognizing how the reciprocity of the universe works can reveal special keys to the nature of the universe. You can participate more fully with the universe if you know how the relationship of reciprocity works. Then, the clear energies of this Stream of Consciousness can be more fully expressed and experienced.

Connecting to the cycles of creation can bring about a new and collaborative energy that understands the complementary force of being within the Universal All. Then, the true knowing that nothing and no one is alone and separate in the world or in the Cosmic All can create the beauty and relatedness that all seek. The Stream of Reciprocity can illuminate a true wisdom of the Divine and bind all people, all situations together. Experiencing this is an epiphany of Divine knowing and the wisdom of mutual cosmology.

The Influences from the Stream of Reciprocity

The energies, qualities and distinguishing perspective from the Stream of Reciprocity reveal the flow of life, consciousness, beauty and spirit in endless collaboration and communication. Reciprocity is a knowing recognition of the interrelatedness of all people, beings, situations, thoughts and life in the presence of the Divine. You may feel an immediate and growing appreciation of the relationships and connections of personal, Universal and Divine exchange. You may feel inspired, generous, grateful and centered in this flow. You may appreciate generosity, compassion, relatedness and caring as vital expressions of the reciprocal flow of life and the Divine.

How may the Stream of Reciprocity influence your life?

Personal Vision inspired by the Stream of Reciprocity

Reciprocity brings a direct knowing of the interrelatedness, communication, participation and collaboration of every aspect of being. It reveals the mutual exchange and connections of all people, beings, places, energies and things. Everything responds and corresponds to everything at some point and possibly at all points. You may feel the reciprocity calling you forward to share good fortune and goodwill as a natural part of your being. You may feel true generosity as a knowing and you are aware of the energies in the world. You are conscious of the Divine, flowing to you and through you and from you in ways that are giving, and knowing and respectful. You may celebrate this rich flow in community and in private, being grateful for all of the flows you know. You may feel a calling to share.

Relatedness inspired by the Stream of Reciprocity

Relatedness inspired by the Stream of Reciprocity reveals how everyone is connected and does share more than is possible to relate. In relationships, this awareness helps bridge ideas, differences, perceptions and concepts into a communication and communal flow. You may be very aware of the give and take in relationships, making sure that generosity and attention is present in your personal and community affiliations. You may be truly present and attentive in your communications to recognize the meaning in conversations and their respective outcomes. You may feel a true kinship with others, knowing the influence, response and mutuality that is present in all things. You may ask others what they want before you ask for yourself, creating a gracious, giving space that recognizes their being. You seek a way of reciprocity so that all people can share in the beauty, blessing and generosity of the world and the Divine. You know the fullness, abundance and infinite gifts that flow in your world and in the Divine All. You are inspired to help, to share, to participate and to celebrate the endless generosity of the All.

World View inspired by the Stream of Reciprocity

Reciprocity in a world view or cosmic view reveals and reinforces the infinite flow of light, of wisdom and of beauty in the Divine. Knowing the reciprocal flow, the loop of energy that always circles and feeds, you are aware of the mutual relatedness of all people, situations, environments and influences. You may experience a bond and communion with all life through this flow of reciprocity, generosity, connectivity and relatedness. You may be inspired to create systems of mutual exchange to connect people to each other for greater benefit. You may see new opportunities to bring communities together that will complement each other in creating a better future. You may coordinate situations and orchestrate the flow so each aspect benefits in the reciprocal alliances.

When you think of reciprocity, when you imagine inspiring co-creative solutions, and generous opportunities and collaborations to uplift your world, what does this inspire in you?

Blessings

The Blessings of the Stream of Reciprocity

May you consciously express the mutual relatedness of life, wisdom, action and blessing.

May you share a greater knowing of the complementary forces within the Universal All.

May you joyfully communicate the replenishing, healing, generous flows of reciprocity.

May you become a shining vessel for Divine communion and interconnection

CHAPTER FIFTEEN:

The Stream of Universality

the all embodying absolute
shares the fullness, the totality, the yes
enhanced by the riches of existence that flow into
the waiting oneness
vibrating omnipresence in the laughing now

The Stream of Universality

The Stream of Universality is a collective resonating frequency that awakens, invites and reveals direct experience and recognition of the Divine in all things and all things in the Divine. This awakens wonder and curiosity. This stream reveals a clear experience of interconnection and the infinite knowing of Divine recognition.

When a person enters and resonates with the Stream of Universality, the profound relationship of the Divine in all, becomes so. The Stream of Universality brings an immediate experience of the pervasive, unlimited presence of the Divine in the All. Those who have experienced the Stream of Universality are awakening, curious, humble and feel in harmony. They perceive and embrace more of their Divine connection and participation with the All.

The Invitation of the Stream of Universality

The Stream of Universality moves steadily, creating a deeper understanding of the nature of place and existence in the world and the great Cosmic All. It is a quiet force of wisdom that appears to infuse everything and everyone. This is a stream of substance and connection. Resonating within this Stream of Consciousness brings an awareness of the essence of life and living. It provides a deeply rooted, yet liberating connection to all consciousness.

The quality of universality is Divine wholeness. It expresses and exudes the principle of pervasiveness. It suggests that which pervades, that which fills all aspects of being. Universality connotes expansive saturation. Life force, life consciousness moves through all of creation, saturating all of creation with an essence of being. This essence of being reveals a commonality, a wholeness that all share. Looking out into the vastness of existence, all share an underlying thread of existence. It is this something that binds all and brings all together in a sense of familiarity. There is something known within each being of consciousness that recognizes and shares consciousness itself. Perhaps universality can best be described as consciousness being aware of consciousness and expressing that underlying awareness.

The Invocation of the Stream of Universality

Vibrationally, the Stream of Universality appears as the undercurrent of vibration. As a frequency it would feel to be the lowest frequency that is barely audible or the highest frequency that is barely audible. The lowest or highest, in this instance, has nothing to do with hierarchy. Higher is no better than lower and visa versa. Universality's range reaches far into the realms of existence, bringing the echoes of knowing together. It is as though through some trick of knowing, that the lowest frequency of sound and light disappears into the highest frequency of sound and light. Each, higher and lower, exists at the furthest ends of the spectrum, and because of this they disappear into each other.

All frequencies move and vibrate, yet feeling for the vibrational pull of this stream is like feeling for the silence. It is a distinguishable resonance, yet remarkably subtle. It feels near. It feels known. It feels indistinguishable, but not unknown. It is the air. One breathes it and through the breathing is aware of its presence. One can feel the wind, but when the air is quiet it is invisible. Universality is presence itself. As presence, it is unrestricted and free in all its associations of being.

One can connect with the qualities of Universality by tuning into the pulse of existence itself. While there is a unique vibration to every aspect of creation, the Stream of Universality reveals a singular pulse of all existence. It is like the principle through which all was conceived, and the substance that is found within and hidden within each aspect of consciousness. This principle or substance, which reveals itself through vibration, allows one to recognize existence or more specifically, the presence of existence. By sensing this vibration, by resonating to the current of this stream, one can feel the commonality of life everywhere.

The Experience of the Stream of Universality

Within the nature of the Stream of Universality is an understanding and appreciation of the quality of a widespread energy. You could call this a Universal principle or the collective knowing of consciousness. The Divine flows through All and all have a clear participation with the Divine. You may not be cognizant of every moment that transpires which reveals the Universe in that moment. Universality is present in every moment, every breath and every aspect of being and the Universality is conscious of the collectivity, connection, influence and omnipresence. The Universality is aware of its immeasurable, infinite influence and participation, as well as its pervasive presence. It is also aware of the details, the flecks, fragments and the factors that create, converge and compose this actualization of the collaboration on individual and collective knowing and being.

An example of this would be standing on a mountain top and viewing the sunrise. You are watching this beauty and you are moved and delighted by the experience. The great sphere of light moves from invisibility to brilliance, illuminating the dark skies with undulating colors. The opacity of the night sky shifts into translucent violets and reds, until the clear blues of a daytime sky and the hot yellow of the sun become evident. As you feel the joy and wonder of this moment, you notice someone else watching the same scene. You smile at the person and that individual smiles back. Nothing is said. Nothing more happens between you.

You have had a mutual experience. Each individual in this example shared the commonality. You participated in the collective energies of the sunrise. You both recognized that mutual experience. It was not simply an experience between two individuals. The sun moved in the skies. This event happened for all of creation. Any being anywhere could feel that event. The sun and the planets moved in the skies and revealed the beauty and brilliance of the Cosmos. Both of you were there to witness it. It was a great moment, a widespread event. In this widespread event, both of you were present. Both of you experienced the presence of that moment. Both of you experienced the prevailing wisdom, the vibrational essence that made that moment universal.

Yet, within this mutual experience is a unique experience as well. From your own view points, each individual had a deeply personal experience. Your own vantage points created something unique inside the event. Within the context of the universal there was something personal. Both of your own understandings were present within the experience. Your own knowing and translation of the event created a personal experience. Each individual felt the sunrise in a different way. Within the universality of the moment, a translation was made. The communal experience also contained an individual knowing.

If each person in this example were to signify a culture, then one culture shared this exact experience with another culture, simultaneously and then each culture moved into its own knowing of that experience. Just like the two individuals viewing the sunrise from the mountain tops, later, each individual went home. They brought their common experience and their individual experience to their own knowing and their own people.

The Stream of Universality spreads a vast field of interrelated vibrations. It underlines a widespread and prevailing knowing. The beauty and wisdom and revelations of the Divine are ever-present, known and experienced.

The Influences from the Stream of Universality

The energies, qualities, vibrations and perspective from the Stream of Universality create a collective wholeness in synchronous appreciation. The connections with all life, all awareness and all wisdom are an expression of Divine inclusivity and creation. This saturation, this pervasive blessing and consciousness is a revelation of belonging, recognition, commonality and gracious appreciation. You may fully recognize your relationship with the universe on a conscious and inner awareness. You may feel your connectivity with a wholeness that feels intimate and also infinite. You may see the wholeness, connection and relatedness in each being you encounter and you celebrate that perspective and gift.

How may the Stream of Universality influence your life?

Personal Vision inspired by the Stream of Universality

Universality is the knowing and experience that everyone and everything is part of the wholeness. The brilliance of each contributes to the brilliance of all. This conscious recognition of universality creates an expansive view of all life and an intimate view of each life. You may feel love permeating all beings as you recognize the Divine love flowing everywhere and in everything. You may be moved by the smallest detail and it resonates throughout life and creates unexpected beauty in the hearts of all. You can feel the flowing relatedness that creates, collaborates and infuses all life in this now. You know the universe flows within you.

Relatedness inspired by the Stream of Universality

Relatedness inspired by the Stream of Universality brings an expanded view of home. Each individual lives in a wholeness home that includes all life and celebrates the magnitude. People in your life share a commonality even if they do not know each other or perceive the world from a similar perspective. You may share personal relationships with those who can grasp and appreciate the expansive nature of each and all and celebrate the prevailing wisdom that all life is part of all life. You may share community relationships with people who are in a more focused attention, while you see and know their contribution is universally felt.

You seek a way of universality so that all people can share the clear and powerful flow of this ever-present knowing of wholeness. Knowing and experiencing this singular pulse, this ultimate relatedness in all people, you hold this knowing for others in all circumstances. You share universality and inclusivity, creating gracious and knowing acceptance for all.

World View inspired by the Stream of Universality

Universality in a world view or cosmic view reveals and reinforces the collective, connection and omnipresence of each individual expression held in wholeness. Individuality and Universality support and reveal the brilliance of each and all. You may feel this interconnection and be inspired and moved by the truth in each being that is contained within the All.

You may create communities to share a collective purpose of beneficial resources that influence the world to create with this focus. You may gather and train leaders to share and develop conscious collective collaborations that uplift the original groups and expand to influence and inspire a new way of perceiving your world. You may break apart preconceived ideas of separateness to embrace related wholeness in honoring, generous and loving ways.

When you think of Universality, when you imagine awakening conscious and mutually beneficial solutions, and generous opportunities and collaborations to uplift your world, what does this inspire in you?

Blessings

The Blessings of the Stream of Universality

May you be an awakening for pervasive
wholeness in the great Cosmic All.

May you be a quiet force of wisdom
through all of creation, who reveals the
commonality each shares.

May you reflect and illuminate a wholeness,
a Life force, a Consciousness
who shines with infinite interconnection.

May you become a vessel for illuminating
the Divine in the All.

CHAPTER SIXTEEN:

The Stream of Unity

all in the totality of One
infinite invitation in the brilliance
of cosmic singularity, one, together, full pulsing
presence of existence
shines an evolving completeness in the fusion of
wholeness

The Stream of Unity

The Stream of Unity is resonating frequency of Oneness that holds direct experience of the totality of the Divine. This awakens peace. This stream reveals a clear experience of cohesiveness, interconnection and presence with the Divine.

When a person enters and resonates with the Stream of Unity, the profound presence of the Divine All, becomes so. The Stream of Unity brings an immediate experience of wholeness. Those who have experienced the Stream of Unity are illuminated, expansive, reverent and feel part of all life. They embrace their Divine connection and recognize the fullness of Being and Oneness.

The Invitation of the Stream of Unity

The Stream of Unity is the declaration of Divine Oneness. It is knowing and recognizing that all things, all essences and all properties are part of a totality. This totality, whatever its makeup, has a flow and substance that links all seemingly separate aspects of itself into a cohesiveness. It is organized into a cohesive entity, recognizable unto itself and complete unto itself.

Each Stream of Consciousness has a quality that distinguishes it as a pathway. The fullness of that quality becomes a beacon of energy, calling forward the essence of that quality and also calling toward it. As one calls forward the essence of the quality, which is the focus of the stream, one is invoking the energies. One is invoking and manifesting the experience and knowing of the focus of that particular stream. As a person calls toward the focus of a stream, they aspire to hold and recognize the energies, experiences and wisdoms created by the energies of that Stream of Consciousness. By participating with the Stream of Unity, one is both calling forward and calling toward the energies and qualities of Unity.

The Invocation of the Stream of Unity

The Stream of Unity is the flow of energy beamed toward this planet which corresponds to the feeling and knowing of Unity, the Oneness of all life, essence and consciousness. This energy of Unity moves in a broad and pervasive manner, infiltrating every aspect of the Cosmic All. Unity connotes a cohesiveness, a binding force that connects each and every particle and consciousness of existence to each other. The patterns of flow throughout the energies of Stream of Unity appear to be a web-like structure, vibrating to a singular frequency and ratio throughout time. This web-like structure connects all aspects of creation. When describing the One or the Stream of Unity, working to understand the structure of this web-like energy is a difficult process.

Since the energy web of Unity connects everything together in a continuous relationship that forms a cohesive whole, then where would the web end and the objects, particles, consciousness and space in between begin? The particles, consciousness and objects are part of the web as a Unity. How do you distinguish the web from the parts it is connecting into a whole?

Since the web is uniting everything, it is part of that union. When the unity of everything is recognized and felt, then the web moves into the wholeness and disappears. The web-like vibrational pattern disappears and seems to dissolve into the Divine Oneness. It is no longer distinguishable. It becomes the Oneness of the Unity that was being described and held. It always was the Oneness, but because the Stream of Unity needed a vibrational resonance to organize itself around, the web-like structure and even the vibrations themselves became the beacon of the experience of Unity.

The Experience of the Stream of Unity

The Stream of Unity is the experience and recognition of Omnipresence. Omnipresence is the pervasive existence of something. This something exists everywhere. There isn't any where, any location, that does not contain this something. There isn't any thing that is missing this something. Whatever else exists in the totality of it all, contains some of this something. Wherever an individual goes, there is some of this something there. Whatever an individual does, there is some of this something in it. It, this something, is everywhere in everything at all times. Naturally, this it, this something, is the Cosmic All, the Goddess, the One, the Divine. Each individual has different words to express the Grand Wholeness, but all recognize that the Divine exists within everything at all times and in all places.

Unity is the Omnipresence of the Divine All. When speaking about existence, you speak about substance, location and time. In order to exist, an object or being needs the organizational substance of the self, a location in geography and a life span. This can be as ephemeral as light or as dense as a planet. Each has an organizational substance, the stuff of itself. Light is organized by its photons and structure. A planet is organized by all of the atomic particles and consciousness that create its form. Both the light and the planet have a location. The planet is located in its sky home. It is revolving around a star somewhere in a particular galaxy. The light is traveling from its original home, the light source, to another location in the universe. Realistically, everything is in motion, whether it appears to be in motion for practical purposes or not. Planet Earth is rotating and revolving around a sun. It has a location in its path of travel. Both the planet and the light have time. They are bound by time and live in time. They have a duration existence as far as human perception is concerned. A planet may exist for millions of years, while a photon may not. Each are defined by the perceptions of existence. Deeper in the field of existence, Unity reveals the wholeness of everything.

Substance, location and time, the indicators of existence, are joined in Unity by an omnipresent vibration. The vibrational resonance of the Stream of Unity is a constant. It is a continual humming, inaudible pattern that permeates all existence while gathering it all into a wholeness. The vibrational resonance can appear to be the binding factor of the Unity. It can also appear to be the by-product of the Unity which already exists in a non-representational form, but appears as a vibrational resonance when it materializes. As a constant, this vibrational resonance moves through time and beyond time. It is a prevailing energy that is always present, always moving and has unlimited existence. Unity as a quality is infinite, unlimited, boundless and continuous. The Stream of Unity beams a vibrational resonance that can reveal this quality and realization to an individual seeking this wisdom.

The search for the experience and knowing of Unity is a human pursuit. Most other consciousnesses know this feeling and truth as a constant. Animals do not feel separated from the Divine. They do not search for the truth or awareness that flows through all of life. They can feel this within themselves. The search for Unity is generally a human or individual consciousness exploration. The Stream of Unity was created to help those individuals who were seized by the yearning to feel the Omnipresence of the Divine One. As they tune into this stream, they become more aligned with that focus and attunement. In resonating more closely with the Unity of all life and all consciousness, the individual would experience the deep communion with the All and the Divine.

The Stream of Unity recognizes the Oneness. Oneness is the singularity. There isn't anything outside of the Oneness. It is whole and total, whether that can be comprehended or not. If you are trying to comprehend the wholeness, then in a certain way, you are separating from the wholeness in order to view it. It is a unique endeavor, but if you are trying to view the wholeness from separation, the wholeness is missing a part of itself. In effect, there is only the knowing that wholeness exists and the individual is a part of that Unity. To experience being part of the Unity of All, you enter the realm of corresponding energies. Each energy corresponds to another energy. You can feel the flow of one piece and the other, moving and vibrating in recognition of their counterpart. As you recognize this aspect of Unity, you then become aware of other energies and aware of the fact that they, too, are moving and flowing in recognition of their counterparts. Soon in this flow of recognition, it is evident that everything vibrates and that vibration corresponds to another vibration somewhere. Within the whole of all of this vibrational awareness, the viewer is participating and influenced by it all. Unity is thus experienced.

The Stream of Unity resonates to a joined focus of Oneness. It invokes the flow and recognition that all substance, all consciousness is part of the Divine All which is a singularity. This singularity contains everything within it. It is an organization of everything into a Unity. Everything that exists, everything that is conscious, everything that was ever created or ever existed is part of this conscious singular essence.

Humanity yearns for the feeling and knowledge of their part in the universe. Humanity wants to know, deep within their being, that they are part of the great beauty and glory of the Cosmic All and the Divine One. Each individual wants to feel the omnipresence of the Divine in their life. They want to feel the interrelatedness of all things and all people. They want to touch the infinite and feel that their life is precious, important and connected to all of creation. The Stream of Unity provides the vibrational patterns that resonate to the celebration of humanity and the celebration of the All.

The Stream of Unity connects with and explores the qualities of Oneness, Wholeness and Interrelatedness. The feeling of Oneness amongst all people helps people understand the cohesive energy that infuses all of humanity with Divine essence and truth. The vibrational flow of this stream can bring an instant sense of familiarity and connection to people. As people participate with this stream, they can feel the true heart to heart energy of humanity and will see and feel the bonds among all people, all animals, all plants and the Cosmic All.

The Influences from the Stream of Unity

The energies, qualities and encompassing perspective from the Stream of Unity reveals the totality of Oneness. This cohesive, united, manifesting flow of Divine resonance brings the essence of separateness into a cohesiveness embrace. All is united. All is included. All is held as One. You may recognize your own individuality and embrace your unique expression of self and the Divine while ensconced in the fullness of the Cosmic All and the Cosmic One. You may experience the Unity and cycle from individual focus into Divine Omnipresence.

How may the Stream of Unity influence your life?

Personal Vision inspired by the Stream of Unity

Unity is revealed as the infinite, unlimited, boundless and continuous expression of all in Oneness. Unity is omnipresent and includes everything into a oneness that may be beyond description, but it is not beyond knowing and experiencing. Your experience of this Unity and Inclusivity may be the epiphany of enlightenment and awakening. You may experience the Grand Wholeness and recognize that the Divine exists within everything at all times and in all places. You may perceive unlimited existence, while knowing your immediate focus and perception. You may celebrate this knowing and feeling as time flows through you from all your lives and experiences to come forward in this moment. You can feel it is so, and this Oneness exists beyond description.

Relatedness inspired by the Stream of Unity

Relatedness inspired by the Stream of Unity reveals the wholeness in life. The brilliance of all created, nurtured, exalted and held in Divine Oneness is breath-taking and real. Each individual contributes to the whole and each individual is part of the whole. You may feel a deeper relatedness to people, animals, places and life through your connection and knowing of unity. You may look into your beloved's eyes and see that person and see the Divine all shining love to you. You may engage with community and see the wholeness in the parts as you honor, appreciate and are truly moved by each contribution. You may be in unity and embrace the flow of everything in the moment and in eternity.

You seek a way of unity so that all people can recognize the relatedness, the beauty and the truth of their individual and collective existence. Knowing, experiencing and sharing this view, this precious container of interrelatedness, you create a way for everyone to know they belong, they are valued and they important to the One and the All.

World View inspired by the Stream of Unity

Unity in a world view or cosmic view reveals the collective Oneness, Wholeness and Interrelatedness of every one, everything, and every expression. You may be moved to create teachings that reveal the interconnectedness of all people and systems that reach across boundaries and imagined separation. You may support people and organizations who celebrate a global view and inclusivity that honors life. You may collect leaders and visionaries to bring together wisdom, respect and generosity in a collaboration that redefines a world view into a true knowing of unity in all people, places, experiences and all life. You may dip into the Unity and create something brilliantly unknown that will reveal the Oneness in us all.

When you think of Unity, when you imagine inspiring heartfelt inclusivity and mutually generous solutions, and unimagined opportunities and collaborations to uplift your world, what does this inspire in you?

Blessings

The Blessings of the Stream of Unity

May you celebrate and embrace Divine connection
and the fullness of Being and Oneness.

May you hold the resonance of the infinite,
unlimited, boundless and continuous
love and being.

May you experience, share and reveal
the realization of Unity in each and every particle
and consciousness of existence.

May you become a clear, uniting vessel for
Oneness with the Divine.

CHAPTER SEVENTEEN:

A Calling Forth

The secrets are now revealed. You have received and accepted your invitation to meet the Streams of Consciousness. Your invitation to meet each stream opens you to great understandings and initial attunements with each individual Stream of Consciousness.

We have described the energies, tunings and gifts of each Stream of Consciousness to you. As you read our words, you have made initial contact. This is a profound revelation to acquaint you with the clear divine flows that have been a gift to you from the Great Beings and the Streams of Consciousness since ancient times. Reading about each Stream of Consciousness is your entry to the experience. Reading the chapters that describe the Streams of Consciousness is more than reading. The frequencies, blessings and wisdom of that stream is present in the words and the pages.

As you encountered and met each stream, you received an introduction and attunement to the blessings of that stream. This is in alignment with your being, your soul, your path and your choice. We, Lumari and I, are honored to have revealed these mysteries and introduce you to the Streams of Consciousness. You may feel an awakening, a recognition and a familiarity with the Streams of Consciousness. You may be more curious and interested in one stream or several streams that seem aligned with your knowing and path today. You may sense that you have had a long affinity with a particular stream and you have a richer understanding of your life path now that you are formally introduced to this stream and to the Streams of Consciousness.

In this moment, look to what you have learned and received. Look to the gifts and openings that each Stream of Consciousness brings you and humanity. Notice and recognize any and all shifts and openings in your perceptions, understanding and personal energy. The shifts and openings may be subtle and they may also create life-changing epiphanies and awakenings. Allow yourself to be with this and explore as you like. The richness of the Streams of Consciousness increases and amplifies.

The Invocation of the Streams of Consciousness

Now, we formally open the way for you to personally encounter the Streams of Consciousness. We open the Invocation, the Calling Forth of the Streams of Consciousness, so you may travel within and have a clear, conscious experience with each stream. This invocation, brings you into harmonious resonance with each stream through a blessing, a meditation and an alignment.

As you read further, as you practice the Chant of Blessing and the Calling Forth of each and any of the Streams of Consciousness, be in the honor, harmony and appreciation with yourself and with the stream. Your invocation opens the Stream of Consciousness to your own soul being and presence. This is your private, individual participation. It aligns you to the stream and to your own sacred vibration in all your beauty. Take your time and give yourself the gift of quietude and attention.

When you choose to go forward and connect with and Call Forth a Stream of Consciousness be in the beauty of your being. Open to each Stream of Consciousness in your timing and grace. Create your own space and practice to be present. As you then learn and engage the Alawashka Chant of Blessing, you will align with the frequencies to Call Forth a Stream of Consciousness. From there, you will engage the ceremony to invoke an individual Stream of Consciousness. This is a journey for you. Honor and celebrate your path and your light.

Start Dancing in the Streams of Consciousness
Get Your Invocations Journey course:
This graceful and powerful audio course, journal and guide, helps you experience, activate and awaken to a clear, harmonious resonance with each of the streams and your connection with the Divine.
Start your journey here Lumari.com

Blessings

May you be open to the blessings of your life.

May you embrace the wisdom, knowing and
frequencies that are a benefit for you.

May the Streams of Consciousness
be a blessing in your life.

CHAPTER EIGHTEEN:

Entering the Stream

E ntering the Streams of Consciousness brings you closer to the Divine in ways that are direct, blessed and in alignment with you.

Engaging in The Alawashka Ceremony and Invocation of the Streams of Consciousness is a direct invitation and connection with a stream to experience those energies in a present, conscious and blessed way. In this section, we bring you a ceremony and invocation to give you direct access to the individual Stream of Consciousness of your choosing. The Alawashka Ceremony and Invocation of the Streams of Consciousness aligns your own being and the stream into a relatedness that is open, conscious and clear.

I am Alawashka and I create the Alawashka Chant of Blessing in my original language of creation for you. We will work with the Alawashka Chant of Blessing to create this greater sacred space and so you may feel and experience an alignment with your inner Divine being and communion with Divine Oneness. I shall explain the energies, and then you may participate in them. I shall explain them from a neutral voice, so Lumari may share this with you. In this you will learn the Alawashka Chant of Blessing, and how to pronounce and chant it, for your greater grace and ease of connection.

Alawashka and the Streams of Consciousness

Alawashka is a celebration of personal and universal joy and abundance. Alawashka is the original language and vibrations frequencies of creation. Alawashka is a fully conscious being, a language that calls creation forth and the flows of energy from the Singular Outpouring. Alawashka reverberates in the highest frequencies. These frequencies are endlessly varied. They work with your own vibrational resonance and help you expand to your next level of being.

The words in Alawashka create. They create that of which they speak. By reading, speaking, singing or listening to the words, the frequencies unfold. Your energetic pattern shifts into one of direct Divine connection. This also occurs within your whole planet. The more you sing or experience Alawashka, the more your personal energies are accelerated. This correlates to shift the energies of all beings on the planet and to the planet Herself. This means that while you are speaking, reading or singing Alawashka, you are also sending this Divine blessing into your world and aligning your world to the All.

The Practice of Invocation

We, Lumari and I, have created a practice of invocation for each Stream of Consciousness, to guide you toward a more gracious, awakening and soul warming journey. The chants and blessings and sacred space preparation help you enter and resonate with each Stream of Consciousness in a way that is uniquely aligned with you, in your multi-dimensional self, and aligned with the specific Stream of Consciousness you have chosen to experience.

The Alawashka Ceremony and Invocation of the Streams of Consciousness

The Alawashka Ceremony and Invocation of the Streams of Consciousness is a way of connecting with each and all of the Streams of Consciousness, to align with your own being, understand the beauty of each stream and lift into new awareness. All of this is created and shared with honor for you, honor for all, and honor for the Divine.

In these practices, we suggest that you first create your quiet, inward, outward, centered space of being.

Begin with the Alawashka Chant Of Blessing.

Read this Chant Of Blessing to align in the highest ways possible for you.

Then, read the Calling Forth of an individual Stream of Consciousness. This will bring you to the opening, so you may experience the gifts of the individual Stream of Consciousness for yourself. Be in a comfortable place that is quiet and undisturbed. You will want your undivided sacred attention to feel all that you feel, notice and perceive.

Allow the grace and blessings of each Stream of Consciousness to flow as it will and in ways that it can best be received.

Entering a Stream of Consciousness

Blessings of the Divine be with You.

This is the practice and blessing to guide you to set the sacred space to engage with the Streams of Consciousness. We create this as blessing, activation and alignment for your most Divine connection.

Prepare yourself with quiet time to create a sacred space. You may have your own centering practices, and we suggest that you do them before you read the individual Stream of

Consciousness chapter. This is a way to set the space for your connection with the Streams of Consciousness.

Move into clear, centered and present attentiveness and flow.
Honor yourself, your energy and your being.
Know that at any time, you may continue being within and resonating with the Stream of Consciousness.
Know that at any time, you may stop this practice.
Take another slow deep breath and center yourself even more.

Once you are clear and centered, you are ready for The Alawashka Chant of Blessing.
Take several deep breaths and chant the words of The Alawashka Chant of Blessing.
You may also look at the Alawashka active sacred geometry image for more attunements.
Every aspect of Alawashka is presented as a gift to you.

The Alawashka Chant of Blessing

The Alawashka Chant of Blessing is a poem that aligns you to receive the blessings, calm and presence of Divine light within.

MAYA SIMA LAKA HO
The living breath is present in the joyous blessing of the soul.

MAYA SIMA LAKA SO
The living breath is the blessing of the soul in joyous oneness.

Pronunciation

MAH'-YAH SEE'-MAH LAH'-KAH HO
MAH'-YAH SEE'-MAH LAH'-KAH SO

Meaning
MAYA is the breath, the Divine inhale and exhale of the All.
SIMA is the greatest joy, a deep rich joy, that can be experienced as bliss.
LAKA is the blessing of the soul, and in this blessing is healing and renewal.
HO is the presence, the now-ness, the here-ness of experience.
SO is the oneness of all awakening and consciousness.

Take several deep breaths and chant the words of The Alawashka Chant of Blessing. You may chant as long as you like to feel the energies, rhythm and blessings. The Alawashka Chant of Blessing helps align your personal being and frequencies with the individual Stream of Consciousness for your most beautiful experience. As you chant these words, allow your essence to feel the opening within. Embrace the abundant flow of highest spirit. Feel the flow of the highest blessings return your embrace. For some, just hearing just one word in Alawashka can create a profound experience of Divine joy and beauty.

When you are ready to engage with the Streams of Consciousness, please, relax yourself in the manner in which you are most comfortable.

Your Invocation to the Stream of Consciousness
After reciting The Alawashka Chant of Blessing, you are attuned to the frequencies of Invitation.
Now, you may open the individual stream with the Streams of Consciousness Invocation.

In this you speak aloud or silently read the special prayer and invocation, and chant the Alawashka word of the stream. This becomes the Calling Forth and creates the most sacred of spaces, alignments and openings for you to experience your chosen Stream of Consciousness.

We have included this practice, so you may see and read The Alawashka Chant of Blessing and the Streams of Consciousness Invocation and move into the beauty and blessing of the Streams of Consciousness.

Blessings

May the Streams of Consciousness bring you blessings for your journey to Divine connection and blessings for your participation in the awakening of humanity and this world.
May the blessings be!

Welcome to the Streams of Consciousness.
You have the opportunity that humanity has been waiting to know and receive.

PART 3

Invocation

Calling Forth and Entering a Stream

CHAPTER NINETEEN:

Invocations and Practices

Invocations are direct requests of the Divine that ask for and bring in specific energies. You are Invoking and Calling Forth a specific Stream of Consciousness to experience the vibrations, wisdom, understanding and reflection of the Divine.

In this section we bring you special practices so you may directly encounter a specific stream and through that, also form a direct personal connection with the Divine. We share guidance and ways of being and holding your energy to create the most aligned experience in this sacred journey. These are two different ways you may engage with this section, Invocation.

The Invocation Practice.

Be in an honoring, centered and clear space.

Choose one stream that speaks to you at this time.

Intone the Alawashka Chant of Blessing to help you align with higher frequencies and set a sacred space.

Formally practice the Invocation, Calling Forth a specific stream.

Let the energies flow. Allow your own process. Be gracious to yourself.

Know when you feel complete, you are complete.

Do the Honoring Disengage practice to return to your more centered present.

Take time to discover and enjoy your experience.

Pay attention to your insights, new opportunities, coincidences and greater understandings that flow and develop for you.

A Read Through

If you prefer to read through this chapter first, without doing a formal invocation, give yourself time to gently experience and understand the Calling Forth for each stream that you read. While you may not be doing a formal invocation, the Stream of Consciousness is present and you may form a strong relationship through reading the invocation. Chanting the name of a stream will form a connection. If you are reading the Calling Forth of a particular stream and you feel a surge of energy or are experiencing an altered focus, you have invoked that stream. It may be best if you allow that experience to unfold, and not continue to read the other invocations and practices. You may also do the Honoring Disengage practice to return to your more centered self. Be present to your self and these energies.

You can also read the chapters, Personal Participation and Entering The Stream to refresh your understanding.

Blessings

Blessing Your Calling Forth

May your Calling Forth
of a Stream of Consciousness
be an enlightening and blessed experience for you.

The Invocation:
Alawashka Chant of Blessing

Blessings of the Divine be with you.
This is a blessing and practice to set the sacred space
for you to engage with the Streams of Consciousness.
We open and awaken the flow of the Streams of Consciousness.
May the blessings flow for you.

Take several deep breaths and say the words of The
Alawashka Chant of Blessing.

You may also look at the Alawashka active sacred geometry
image for more attunements.
Now it is time to open set the sacred space for you to engage
with the Streams of Consciousness.

Please, relax yourself in the manner in which you are most
comfortable.

Alawashka Chant of Blessing

Take a slow deep breath.
Feel the breath rise and fall within you.
Take another deep breath.
Imagine that this breath is a long shimmering thread that
extends from the Heart of the Universe to you.
Take another slow deep breath and feel this thread, which
is permeated with light, joy, and sparkling energies, fill you
with the grace of being.

Chant the words of The Alawashka Chant of Blessing and feel
a shift in your attention and energy.

Maya Sima Laka Ho. ~ Maya Sima Laka So.
Maya Sima Laka Ho. ~ Maya Sima Laka So.
Maya Sima Laka Ho. ~ Maya Sima Laka So.
Maya Sima Laka Ho. ~ Maya Sima Laka So.
Maya Sima Laka Ho. ~ Maya Sima Laka So.

Now, Take a slow deep breath.
Feel the breath rise and fall within you.
Now say,
I honor my path, my calling and my being in all directions.
I honor the wisdom, vibrations and experiences set forth in
the Stream of Consciousness.
I honor and accept the invitation to enter Streams of
Consciousness.
The Alawashka Chant of Blessing is complete and whole.

Take another slow deep breath and when you are ready,
read the chapter for one specific Stream of Consciousness.
Listen for the words of guidance that may come to you.
Be open to hear or receive a greater understanding of your
own Divinity and Life.

Bless you for you are more than you know.

The Invocation:
Calling Forth the Stream of Purity
~ Anyata ~

The Stream of Purity

This is an invocation and ceremony to set the sacred space for you to engage with the Stream of Purity ~ Anyata. (Pronounced   AHN – YAH' – TAH)

We invite you to include The Alawashka Chant of Blessing to expand and synchronize your energy.

Please, relax and center yourself in the manner in which you are most comfortable.

Take a slow, deep breath.
Honor your path, calling and being.
Honor the wisdom and vibrations set forth in the Stream of Purity.

Honor the invitation to receive the blessings of the Stream of Purity.

Take a slow deep breath.
Center yourself and read.

The Stream of Purity brings the high vibrations of Divine clarity to awaken a pure, unfiltered, direct experience of the Divine. The energies from this stream bring continual openings and alignments to each individual, so you may encounter the true Divine Oneness in the most optimal way. With this focus and activation, you can clear the pathways to resonate in the appropriate manner for your personal, authentic connection and relationship with the Divine and create a pure connection with all life.

Take a slow deep breath. Center yourself.
Tune into the Stream of Purity.
Gently open to receive the blessings of the Stream of Purity in elegant alignment with your being.
Pause, breathe and receive.

Calling Forth the Stream of Purity
Now we begin.
We open and awaken the flow of the Stream of Purity and may the blessings flow for you.

Now, take a slow deep breath. Feel the breath rise and fall within you.
Chant the Awakening of the Stream of Purity.

Anyata ~ Anyata ~ Anyata
Anyata ~ Anyata ~ Anyata ~ Anyata
Anyata ~ Anyata ~ Anyata ~ Anyata ~ Anyata
~ Anyata ~

Take another deep breath and connect with the Stream of Purity, now.
Feel the opening and invitation to proceed.

Be open to hear or receive a greater understanding of your own Divinity.
Listen for the words of guidance that may come to you.
Pause and take as much time as benefits you.

When you feel complete, then you are complete.

Take a slow deep breath. Center yourself.
Move into centered focus and say, *"Thank you."*

Take a slow, deep breath. Center yourself
Pause, breathe and receive.

Take a slow, deep breath. Center yourself
Pause, breathe and perceive.

Take a slow, deep breath. Center yourself
Pause, breathe and conceive.

Be present to this moment and breathe your soul.

Blessings of the Divine be with you.

Bless you for you are more than you know.

The Invocation:
Calling Forth the Stream of Honor
~ Halle ~

The Stream of Honor

This is an invocation and ceremony to set the sacred space for you to engage with the Stream of Honor ~ Halle.
(Pronounced   HAH' – LAY)

We invite you to include The Alawashka Chant of Blessing to expand and synchronize your energy.

Please, relax and center yourself in the manner in which you are most comfortable.

Take a slow, deep breath.
Honor your path, calling and being.
Honor the wisdom and vibrations set forth in the Stream of Honor.

Honor the invitation to receive the blessings of the Stream of Honor.

Take a slow deep breath.
Center yourself and read.

The Stream of Honor generates the spiritual vibrations of appreciation, reverence, respect and acknowledgment to oneself, to another and to the Divine. With the quality of honor, each individual can feel and know their life as a contribution to all of creation. Each individual can understand and recognize the true importance of others. With the extension of honor to all life, the reverence for life will be felt in every moment.

Take a slow deep breath. Center yourself.
Tune into the Stream of Honor.
Gently open to receive the blessings of the Stream of Honor
in elegant alignment with your being.
Pause, breathe and receive.

Calling Forth the Stream of Honor

Now we begin.
We open and awaken the flow of the Stream of Honor and may the blessings flow for you.

Now, take a slow deep breath. Feel the breath rise and fall within you.
Chant the Awakening of the Stream of Honor.

Halle ~ Halle ~ Halle
Halle ~ Halle ~ Halle ~ Halle
Halle ~ Halle ~ Halle ~ Halle ~ Halle

Take another deep breath and connect with the Stream of Honor, now.
Feel the opening and invitation to proceed.

Be open to hear or receive a greater understanding of your own Divinity.
Listen for the words of guidance that may come to you.
Pause and take as much time as benefits you.

When you feel complete, then you are complete.

Take a slow deep breath. Center yourself.
Move into centered focus and say, *"Thank you."*

Take a slow, deep breath. Center yourself
Pause, breathe and receive.

Take a slow, deep breath. Center yourself
Pause, breathe and perceive.

Take a slow, deep breath. Center yourself
Pause, breathe and conceive.

Be present to this moment and breathe your soul.

Blessings of the Divine be with you.

Bless you for you are more than you know.

The Invocation:
Calling Forth the Stream of
Compassion
~ Onwatu ~

The Stream of Compassion

This is an invocation and ceremony to set the sacred space for you to engage with the Stream of Compassion ~ Onwatu. (Pronounced   OHN – WAH' – TU)

We invite you to include The Alawashka Chant of Blessing to expand and synchronize your energy.

Please, relax and center yourself in the manner in which you are most comfortable.

Take a slow, deep breath.
Honor your path, calling and being.
Honor the wisdom and vibrations set forth in the Stream of Compassion.

Honor the invitation to receive the blessings of the Stream of Compassion.

Take a slow deep breath.
Center yourself and read.

The Stream of Compassion brings profound understanding and empathy for everyone and everything. This compassion comes from the knowing of the shared kinship in all things. Deep consideration, connection and even devotion resonates within the individual. By extending and feeling that compassion for the lives and experiences of all beings, a great relatedness with all creation is evident.

Take a slow deep breath. Center yourself.
Tune into the Stream of Compassion.
Gently open to receive the blessings of the Stream of Compassion in elegant alignment with your being.
Pause, breathe and receive.

Calling Forth the Stream of Compassion
Now we begin.
We open and awaken the flow of the Stream of Compassion and may the blessings flow for you.

Now, take a slow deep breath. Feel the breath rise and fall within you.
Chant the Awakening of the Stream of Compassion.

Onwatu ~ Onwatu ~ Onwatu
Onwatu ~ Onwatu ~ Onwatu ~ Onwatu
Onwatu ~ Onwatu ~ Onwatu ~ Onwatu ~ Onwatu

Take another deep breath and connect with the Stream of Compassion, now.
Feel the opening and invitation to proceed.

Be open to hear or receive a greater understanding of your own Divinity.
Listen for the words of guidance that may come to you.
Pause and take as much time as benefits you.

When you feel complete, then you are complete.

Take a slow deep breath. Center yourself.
Move into centered focus and say, *"Thank you."*

Take a slow, deep breath. Center yourself
Pause, breathe and receive.

Take a slow, deep breath. Center yourself
Pause, breathe and perceive.

Take a slow, deep breath. Center yourself
Pause, breathe and conceive.

Be present to this moment and breathe your soul.

Blessings of the Divine be with you.

Bless you for you are more than you know.

The Invocation:
Calling Forth the Stream of Neutrality
~ Makasa ~

The Stream of Neutrality

This is an invocation and ceremony to set the sacred space for you to engage with the Stream of Neutrality ~ Makasa. (Pronounced   MAH - KAH '- SAH)

We invite you to include The Alawashka Chant of Blessing to expand and synchronize your energy.

Please, relax and center yourself in the manner in which you are most comfortable.

Take a slow, deep breath.
Honor your path, calling and being.

Honor the wisdom and vibrations set forth in the Stream of Neutrality.
Honor the invitation to receive the blessings of the Stream of Neutrality.

Take a slow deep breath.
Center yourself and read.

The Stream of Neutrality brings a balance and a deep appreciation of equality and sacred impartiality. Through this clarity, a true sense of centeredness holds all of the perceptions in a calm wholeness. This clear vision reflects an equanimity for all life. All is important and an integral aspect of the Divine and the All. Nothing is higher or lower, therefore no one is more favored or less valued. Each person and being is recognized, considered and valued.

Take a slow deep breath. Center yourself.
Tune into the Stream of Neutrality.
Gently open to receive the blessings of the Stream of
Neutrality in elegant alignment with your being.
Pause, breathe and receive.

Calling Forth the Stream of Neutrality
Now we begin.
We open and awaken the flow of the Stream of Neutrality and may the blessings flow for you.

Now, take a slow deep breath. Feel the breath rise and fall within you.
Chant the Awakening of the Stream of Neutrality.

Makasa ~ Makasa ~ Makasa
Makasa ~ Makasa ~ Makasa ~ Makasa
Makasa ~ Makasa ~ Makasa ~ Makasa ~ Makasa

Take another deep breath and connect with the Stream of Neutrality, now.
Feel the opening and invitation to proceed.

Be open to hear or receive a greater understanding of your own Divinity.
Listen for the words of guidance that may come to you.
Pause and take as much time as benefits you.

When you feel complete, then you are complete.

Take a slow deep breath. Center yourself.
Move into centered focus and say, *"Thank you."*

Take a slow, deep breath. Center yourself
Pause, breathe and receive.

Take a slow, deep breath. Center yourself
Pause, breathe and perceive.

Take a slow, deep breath. Center yourself
Pause, breathe and conceive.

Be present to this moment and breathe your soul.

Blessings of the Divine be with you.

Bless you for you are more than you know.

The Invocation:
Calling Forth the Stream of Harmony
~ Wanshatta ~

The Stream of Harmony

This is an invocation and ceremony to set the sacred space for you to engage with the Stream of Harmony ~ Wanshatta. (Pronounced   WAHN - SHAH' – TAH)

We invite you to include The Alawashka Chant of Blessing to expand and synchronize your energy.

Please, relax and center yourself in the manner in which you are most comfortable.

Take a slow, deep breath.
Honor your path, calling and being.
Honor the wisdom and vibrations set forth in the Stream of Harmony.

Honor the invitation to receive the blessings of the Stream of Harmony.

Take a slow deep breath.
Center yourself and read.

The Stream of Harmony resonates to the interrelatedness of all beings, all situations and all portions of the Divine. This is seen and known as a collaborative expression, each individual energy blending with every other in a related melodious flow. Every aspect of life adapts to and makes room for the others, so that each voice can be heard, recognized and welcomed. The resonance of harmony appreciates and seeks out all voices so that each is included in the whole.

Take a slow deep breath. Center yourself.
Tune into the Stream of Harmony.
Gently open to receive the blessings of the Stream of Harmony in elegant alignment with your being.
Pause, breathe and receive.

Calling Forth the Stream of Harmony
Now we begin.
We open and awaken the flow of the Stream of Harmony and may the blessings flow for you.

Now, take a slow deep breath. Feel the breath rise and fall within you.
Chant the Awakening of the Stream of Harmony.

Wanshatta ~ Wanshatta ~ Wanshatta
Wanshatta ~ Wanshatta ~ Wanshatta ~ Wanshatta
Wanshatta ~ Wanshatta ~ Wanshatta ~ Wanshatta
~ Wanshatta ~

Take another deep breath and connect with the Stream of Harmony, now.
Feel the opening and invitation to proceed.

Be open to hear or receive a greater understanding of your own Divinity.
Listen for the words of guidance that may come to you.
Pause and take as much time as benefits you.

When you feel complete, then you are complete.

Take a slow deep breath. Center yourself.
Move into centered focus and say, *"Thank you."*

Take a slow, deep breath. Center yourself
Pause, breathe and receive.

Take a slow, deep breath. Center yourself
Pause, breathe and perceive.

Take a slow, deep breath. Center yourself
Pause, breathe and conceive.

Be present to this moment and breathe your soul.

Blessings of the Divine be with you.

Bless you for you are more than you know.

The Invocation: Calling Forth the Stream of Beauty and Grace
~ Wanaka ~

The Stream of Beauty and Grace

This is an invocation and ceremony to set the sacred space for you to engage with the Stream of Beauty and Grace ~ Wanaka. (Pronounced   WAH - NAH' - KAH)

We invite you to include The Alawashka Chant of Blessing to expand and synchronize your energy.

Please, relax and center yourself in the manner in which you are most comfortable.

Take a slow, deep breath.
Honor your path, calling and being.
Honor the wisdom and vibrations set forth in the Stream of Beauty and Grace.

Honor the invitation to receive the blessings of the Stream of Beauty and Grace.

Take a slow deep breath.
Center yourself and read.

The Stream of Beauty and Grace reveals the appreciation, awe and delight in and of all things. This inspirational perspective awakens the expression and connection of Divine creation in One and All. The Stream of Beauty and Grace recognizes and values each person's individual gifts and expressions as direct pathway of continual relationship with Divine Source. To know and perceive beauty and grace is a gift of splendor to everyone, which continues throughout awareness and celebrates this within all creation.

Take a slow deep breath. Center yourself.
Tune into the Stream of Beauty and Grace.
Gently open to receive the blessings of the Stream of Beauty and Grace in elegant alignment with your being.
Pause, breathe and receive.

Calling Forth the Stream of Beauty and Grace
Now we begin.
We open and awaken the flow of the Stream of Beauty and Grace and may the blessings flow for you.

Now, take a slow deep breath. Feel the breath rise and fall within you.
Chant the Awakening of the Stream of Beauty and Grace.

Wanaka ~ Wanaka ~ Wanaka
Wanaka ~ Wanaka ~ Wanaka ~ Wanaka
Wanaka ~ Wanaka ~ Wanaka ~ Wanaka ~ Wanaka

Take another deep breath and connect with the Stream of Beauty and Grace, now.
Feel the opening and invitation to proceed.

Be open to hear or receive a greater understanding of your own Divinity.
Listen for the words of guidance that may come to you.
Pause and take as much time as benefits you.

When you feel complete, then you are complete.

Take a slow deep breath. Center yourself.
Move into centered focus and say, *"Thank you."*

Take a slow, deep breath. Center yourself
Pause, breathe and receive.

Take a slow, deep breath. Center yourself
Pause, breathe and perceive.

Take a slow, deep breath. Center yourself
Pause, breathe and conceive.

Be present to this moment and breathe your soul.

Blessings of the Divine be with you.

Bless you for you are more than you know.

The Invocation:
Calling Forth the Stream of Wisdom
~ Asicka ~

The Stream of Wisdom

This is an invocation and ceremony to set the sacred space for you to engage with the Stream of Wisdom ~ Asicka. (Pronounced   AH - SEE' – KAH)

We invite you to include The Alawashka Chant of Blessing to expand and synchronize your energy.

Please, relax and center yourself in the manner in which you are most comfortable.

Take a slow, deep breath.
Honor your path, calling and being.
Honor the wisdom and vibrations set forth in the Stream of Wisdom.

Honor the invitation to receive the blessings of the Stream of
Wisdom.

Take a slow deep breath.
Center yourself and read.

The Stream of Wisdom holds the memory of the ancients
and the knowing of now. Every cycle and event is a rhythm
contained within the deep memory of wisdom. In this stream's
resonance, nothing is lost. Every thought, action and event
has been held, cherished and contained, because every event,
every person's life, is a rich contribution to the wholeness of
life. This stream shows each person how vital and important
their entire existence is to the whole of life.

Take a slow deep breath. Center yourself.
Tune into the Stream of Wisdom.
Gently open to receive the blessings of the Stream of
Wisdom in elegant alignment with your being.
Pause, breathe and receive.

Calling Forth the Stream of Wisdom
Now we begin.
We open and awaken the flow of the Stream of Wisdom and
may the blessings flow for you.

Now, take a slow deep breath. Feel the breath rise and fall
within you.
Chant the Awakening of the Stream of Wisdom.

Asicka ~ Asicka ~ Asicka
Asicka ~ Asicka ~ Asicka ~ Asicka
Asicka ~ Asicka ~ Asicka ~ Asicka ~ Asicka

Take another deep breath and connect with the Stream of Wisdom, now.
Feel the opening and invitation to proceed.

Be open to hear or receive a greater understanding of your own Divinity.
Listen for the words of guidance that may come to you.
Pause and take as much time as benefits you.

When you feel complete, then you are complete.

Take a slow deep breath. Center yourself.
Move into centered focus and say, *"Thank you."*

Take a slow, deep breath. Center yourself
Pause, breathe and receive.

Take a slow, deep breath. Center yourself
Pause, breathe and perceive.

Take a slow, deep breath. Center yourself
Pause, breathe and conceive.

Be present to this moment and breathe your soul.

Blessings of the Divine be with you.

Bless you for you are more than you know.

The Invocation:
Calling Forth the Stream of Truth
~ Seela ~

The Stream of Truth

This is an invocation and ceremony to set the sacred space for you to engage with the Stream of Truth ~ Seela. (Pronounced   SEE'- LAH)

We invite you to include The Alawashka Chant of Blessing to expand and synchronize your energy.

Please, relax and center yourself in the manner in which you are most comfortable.

Take a slow, deep breath.
Honor your path, calling and being.
Honor the Truth and, vibrations set forth in the Stream of Truth.

Honor the invitation to receive the blessings of the Stream of Truth.

Take a slow deep breath.
 Center yourself and read.

The Stream of Truth acknowledges the fundamental core of all life. The Stream of Truth resonates to the essential and underlying core of life and reveals the deepest knowing and understanding of one's experience and essence. As truth shines forward, all perspectives are clear and all confusions are eliminated. Every individual can let go of their own confusion and be exactly who they are and grand awakenings continue to take place.

Take a slow deep breath. Center yourself.
Tune into the Stream of Truth.
Gently open to receive the blessings of the Stream of Truth
in elegant alignment with your being.
Pause, breathe and receive.

Calling Forth the Stream of Truth

Now we begin.
We open and awaken the flow of the Stream of Truth and may the blessings flow for you.

Now, take a slow deep breath. Feel the breath rise and fall within you.
Chant the Awakening of the Stream of Truth.

Seela ~ Seela ~ Seela
Seela ~ Seela ~ Seela ~ Seela
Seela ~ Seela ~ Seela ~ Seela ~ Seela

Take another deep breath and connect with the Stream of Truth, now.
Feel the opening and invitation to proceed.

Be open to hear or receive a greater understanding of your own Divinity.
Listen for the words of guidance that may come to you.
Pause and take as much time as benefits you.

When you feel complete, then you are complete.

Take a slow deep breath. Center yourself.
Move into centered focus and say, *"Thank you."*

Take a slow, deep breath. Center yourself
Pause, breathe and receive.

Take a slow, deep breath. Center yourself
Pause, breathe and perceive.

Take a slow, deep breath. Center yourself
Pause, breathe and conceive.

Be present to this moment and breathe your soul.

Blessings of the Divine be with you.

Bless you for you are more than you know.

The Invocation:
Calling Forth the Stream of Radiance
~ Amato ~

The Stream of Radiance

This is an invocation and ceremony to set the sacred space for
you to engage with the Stream of Radiance ~ Amato.
(Pronounced   AH- MAH' – TOE)

We invite you to include The Alawashka Chant of Blessing to
expand and synchronize your energy.

Please, relax and center yourself in the manner in which you
are most comfortable.

Take a slow, deep breath.
Honor your path, calling and being.
Honor the Radiance, and the vibrations set forth in the Stream
of Radiance.

Honor the invitation to receive the blessings of the Stream of Radiance.

Take a slow deep breath.
 Center yourself and read.

The Stream of Radiance vibrantly illuminates a clear, awakening that all Divine wisdom and human consciousness is revered. Light Divinely shines and generosity, understanding and reflection shine forward and inward. It combines personal, global and universal aspects in this expanded awakening and brings them together in a view of wholeness and appreciation. The resplendent light herein, declares that true wealth is the radiance of Divine spirit which fills everyone and everything.

Take a slow deep breath. Center yourself.
Tune into the Stream of Radiance.
Gently open to receive the blessings of the Stream of
Radiance in elegant alignment with your being.
Pause, breathe and receive.

Calling Forth the Stream of Radiance
Now we begin.
We open and awaken the flow of the Stream of Radiance and may the blessings flow for you.

Now, take a slow deep breath. Feel the breath rise and fall within you.
Chant the Awakening of the Stream of Radiance.

Amato ~ Amato ~ Amato
Amato ~ Amato ~ Amato ~ Amato
Amato ~ Amato ~ Amato ~ Amato ~ Amato

Take another deep breath and connect with the Stream of Radiance, now.
Feel the opening and invitation to proceed.

Be open to hear or receive a greater understanding of your own Divinity.
Listen for the words of guidance that may come to you.
Pause and take as much time as benefits you.

When you feel complete, then you are complete.

Take a slow deep breath. Center yourself.
Move into centered focus and say, *"Thank you."*

Take a slow, deep breath. Center yourself
Pause, breathe and receive.

Take a slow, deep breath. Center yourself
Pause, breathe and perceive.

Take a slow, deep breath. Center yourself
Pause, breathe and conceive.

Be present to this moment and breathe your soul.

Blessings of the Divine be with you.

Bless you for you are more than you know.

The Invocation:
Calling Forth the Stream of Reciprocity
~ Munaka ~

The Stream of Reciprocity

This is an invocation and ceremony to set the sacred space for you to engage with the Stream of Reciprocity ~ Munaka.
(Pronounced   MOO- NAH'- KAH)

We invite you to include The Alawashka Chant of Blessing to expand and synchronize your energy.

Please, relax and center yourself in the manner in which you are most comfortable.

Take a slow, deep breath.
Honor your path, calling and being.
Honor the Reciprocity, and vibrations set forth in the Stream of Reciprocity.

Honor the invitation to receive the blessings of the Stream of Reciprocity.

Take a slow deep breath.
Center yourself and read.
The Stream of Reciprocity proclaims the pervasive flow of mutual exchange. Nothing is separate from its influence upon other things. Reciprocity reveals that everything responds and corresponds to everything else and all are interrelated. All are appreciated and recognized. Each is vital and responsible for themselves, each other and the whole. In this Divine expression, the interconnected flow reveals itself and shines in each one.

Take a slow deep breath. Center yourself.
Tune into the Stream of Reciprocity.
Gently open to receive the blessings of the Stream of
Reciprocity in elegant alignment with your being.
Pause, breathe and receive.

Calling Forth the Stream of Reciprocity

Now we begin.
We open and awaken the flow of the Stream of Reciprocity and may the blessings flow for you.

Now, take a slow deep breath. Feel the breath rise and fall within you.
Chant the Awakening of the Stream of Reciprocity.

Munaka ~ Munaka ~ Munaka
Munaka ~ Munaka ~ Munaka ~ Munaka
Munaka ~ Munaka ~ Munaka ~ Munaka ~ Munaka

Take another deep breath and connect with the Stream of Reciprocity, now.
Feel the opening and invitation to proceed.

Be open to hear or receive a greater understanding of your own Divinity.
Listen for the words of guidance that may come to you.
Pause and take as much time as benefits you.

When you feel complete, then you are complete.

Take a slow deep breath. Center yourself.
Move into centered focus and say, *"Thank you."*

Take a slow, deep breath. Center yourself
Pause, breathe and receive.

Take a slow, deep breath. Center yourself
Pause, breathe and perceive.

Take a slow, deep breath. Center yourself
Pause, breathe and conceive.

Be present to this moment and breathe your soul.

Blessings of the Divine be with you.

Bless you for you are more than you know.

The Invocation:
Calling Forth the Stream of Universality
~ Hanuka ~

The Stream of Universality

This is an invocation and ceremony to set the sacred space for you to engage with the Stream of Universality ~ Hanuka.
(Pronounced   HAH- NOO'- KAH)

We invite you to include The Alawashka Chant of Blessing to expand and synchronize your energy.

Please, relax and center yourself in the manner in which you are most comfortable.

Take a slow, deep breath.
Honor your path, calling and being.
Honor the Universality, and vibrations set forth in the Stream of Universality.

Honor the invitation to receive the blessings of the Stream of Universality.

Take a slow deep breath.
Center yourself and read.

The Stream of Universality is wholeness. It resonates the profound truth that the Divine fills all aspects of being. It is the recognition of the Divine in all things and all things in the Divine. Therefore, each person is Divine and is part of the All. Experiencing this universality gives immediate experience of the pervasive, unlimited presence of the Divine in the All. Each and every person, being and essence is alive and cherished in the wholeness of all-embracing, all-inclusive life.

Take a slow deep breath. Center yourself.
Tune into the Stream of Universality.
Gently open to receive the blessings of the Stream of Universality in elegant alignment with your being.
Pause, breathe and receive.

Calling Forth the Stream of Universality
Now we begin.
We open and awaken the flow of the Stream of Universality and may the blessings flow for you.

Now, take a slow deep breath. Feel the breath rise and fall within you.
Chant the Awakening of the Stream of Universality.

Hanuka ~ Hanuka ~ Hanuka
Hanuka ~ Hanuka ~ Hanuka ~ Hanuka
Hanuka ~ Hanuka ~ Hanuka ~ Hanuka ~ Hanuka

Take another deep breath and connect with the Stream of Universality, now.
Feel the opening and invitation to proceed.

Be open to hear or receive a greater understanding of your own Divinity.
Listen for the words of guidance that may come to you.
Pause and take as much time as benefits you.

When you feel complete, then you are complete.

Take a slow deep breath. Center yourself.
Move into centered focus and say, *"Thank you."*

Take a slow, deep breath. Center yourself
Pause, breathe and receive.

Take a slow, deep breath. Center yourself
Pause, breathe and perceive.

Take a slow, deep breath. Center yourself
Pause, breathe and conceive.

Be present to this moment and breathe your soul.

Blessings of the Divine be with you.

Bless you for you are more than you know.

The Invocation:
Calling Forth the Stream of Unity
~ Haroko ~

The Stream of Unity

This is an invocation and ceremony to set the sacred space for
you to engage with the Stream of Unity ~ Haroko.
(Pronounced   HAH- ROE'- KOE)

We invite you to include The Alawashka Chant of Blessing to
expand and synchronize your energy.

Please, relax and center yourself in the manner in which you
are most comfortable.

Take a slow, deep breath.
Honor your path, calling and being.
Honor the Unity, and vibrations set forth in the Stream of Unity.

Honor the invitation to receive the blessings of the Stream of Unity.

Take a slow deep breath.
Center yourself and read.

The Stream of Unity is the revelation of Oneness. It reveals that all things, all essences and all properties are part of a totality. Every aspect, every essence, every configuration, including all of life, reveals the Oneness of all and the Divine. Each person, no matter what their circumstances or beliefs, is an integral, appreciated and celebrated part of this Oneness. In this great Oneness, limitations and boundaries fade. Unity is revealed as whole, complete and singularly Divine.

Take a slow deep breath. Center yourself.
Tune into the Stream of Unity.
Gently open to receive the blessings of the Stream of Unity
in elegant alignment with your being.
Pause, breathe and receive.

Calling Forth the Stream of Unity

Now we begin.
We open and awaken the flow of the Stream of Unity and may the blessings flow for you.

Now, Take a slow deep breath. Feel the breath rise and fall within you.
Chant the Awakening of the Stream of Unity.

Haroko ~ Haroko ~ Haroko
Haroko ~ Haroko ~ Haroko ~ Haroko
Haroko ~ Haroko ~ Haroko ~ Haroko ~ Haroko

Take another deep breath and connect with the Stream of
Unity, now.
Feel the opening and invitation to proceed.

Be open to hear or receive a greater understanding of your
own Divinity.
Listen for the words of guidance that may come to you.
Pause and take as much time as benefits you.

When you feel complete, then you are complete.

Take a slow deep breath. Center yourself.
Move into centered focus and say, *"Thank you."*

Take a slow, deep breath. Center yourself
Pause, breathe and receive.

Take a slow, deep breath. Center yourself
Pause, breathe and perceive.

Take a slow, deep breath. Center yourself
Pause, breathe and conceive.

Be present to this moment and breathe your soul.

Blessings of the Divine be with you.

Bless you for you are more than you know.

~ Create An Honoring Disengage ~

Now, when you are ready to leave a Stream of Consciousness, it's beneficial to create an honoring disengage. An honoring disengage is a practice to thank and acknowledge the blessings of that Stream of Consciousness. Then you move more into a personal wholeness and focus. This allows you to understand and experience the wisdom and gifts of the stream and be centered and present in your everyday life.

When you create honoring disengage, you say a deep and profound thank you. You release the connections and focus of that stream. You tune into your own personal focus.

Then you move into the now of your life.

The Practice of Honoring Disengage

Take a slow deep breath.

Center yourself.

Feel into and acknowledge the gifts you have received from aligning with this Stream of Consciousness.

Breathe in the gifts. Feel the energy shifts and attunements.

Acknowledge any and all healing, insights, revelations and advanced perspectives.

Give yourself time to appreciate your personal experience in this Stream of Consciousness.

Take a slow deep breath.

Now, say thank you.

Thank you, Divine Ones, thank you Stream of Consciousness for the beauty and resonance and revelations of this stream.

I honor you for sharing these gifts. I honor my new wisdom and knowing.

I honor the sacred now and I honor my being.

I am in appreciation and recognition.

In this moment, I move into a space of my wholeness.

In this moment, I am letting go of the deep connection with this stream to appreciate, understand and integrate these blessings in my being and my life.

Thank you. Thank you. Thank you.

Take another slow, deep breath. Center yourself.

And so it is.

And so it shall be.

Now you may think about, journal and reflect upon the energies, gifts, insights, wisdom and transformations you received.

~ Create An Honoring Acknowledgement ~

Y ou have connected with the Streams Of Consciousness in more intimate and knowing ways. Sometimes, encountering the Streams of Consciousness awakens memories and greater awareness of your past and past lives. You may see, feel and remember lives where you were kind, in harmony and created benefit to many. You lived in an alignment with your personal Stream of Consciousness.

While encountering the Streams of Consciousness, you may also have experienced or recognized past situations where your own thoughts, assumptions or actions did not bring harmony, love, caring and create benefit to many. Many individuals have a past that has aspects that are brilliant and aspects that have shadows. How do you acknowledge and address these actions as you perceive them now?

We have created an Honoring Acknowledgement practice to help you in this regard. In this Honoring Acknowledgement practice, you may shift into knowing and recognition, to release the energies of misunderstandings, misconduct and misdoings. Please know that we created this Honoring Acknowledgement practice for those of you who feel moved by your past, so you may have a powerful realignment now. You do not need to feel obligated to do this Honoring Acknowledgement practice. We simply felt that if you encountered and remembered lifetime experiences that were not beneficial, that this practice, would help you in many ways.

An Honoring Acknowledgement is a practice of recognition and acknowledgement of the actions, conversations or situations from your life and past, that are not your highest expression and may have caused harm.

When you create Honoring Acknowledgement, you are in recognition of your past, and you declare a deep and profound acknowledgement of the actions, conversations or situations that may have caused harm. This is an offering of sincerity for what you can understand and also what may have unfolded beyond your understanding. You respectfully accept the impact for those thoughts, assumptions or actions. Then, you release the energies that are still connected with those misunderstandings, misconducts and misdoings from you. In completion, you move into the now of your life and tune into your own personal focus.

Of course, if this is personal and if this occurred in this lifetime, you may make amends if it is appropriate. If you feel moved to send an Honoring Acknowledgement, because of instances from other lifetimes, this is a beautiful practice for you.

Simply remember this is an honoring act and you are releasing the flow. This is not to burden you or ask you to accept responsibility for all thoughts and misdeeds in your past, for all thoughts and misdeeds in your world and for all thoughts and misdeeds in beyond. Your Honoring Acknowledgement brings an integrity of wholeness.

The Practice of Honoring Acknowledgement

Take a slow deep breath.

Center yourself.

Breathe in and recognize your own deeper understanding of your life and of life that has occurred in this world.

Acknowledge any and all healing, insights, revelations and advanced perspectives you have at this time.

Give yourself time to appreciate your personal experience in this Stream of Consciousness.

Give yourself time to appreciate your new insight that leads you to create an Honoring Acknowledgement.

Take a moment and understand any misunderstandings, misconduct and misdoings that have created shadows for you and / or for others.

Simply recognize, acknowledge and accept that you were in some way involved.

Take a slow deep breath, and say

"I recognize the misunderstandings, misconduct and misdoings that have created shadows for others and for myself. In this sacred space right now, I offer my sincere and true acknowledgement, responsibility and acceptance. In my sincere and true acknowledgement, responsibility and acceptance, I release my connection and contribution to these acts of misconduct, misdoing and misunderstanding."

Take a slow deep breath, and release.

Release the energy, sorrow, confusion, annoyance, guilt, fear, sadness, anger and regret.

Now say, "In my sincere and true acknowledgement, responsibility and acceptance, I release my connection and contribution to any acts of misconduct, misdoing and misunderstanding."

Take a slow deep breath, and release.
Release the energy, sorrow, confusion, annoyance, guilt, fear, sadness, anger and regret.

Take another slow deep breath, and say
"In this moment, I am letting go and releasing this Honoring Acknowledgement."
"May wholeness and blessing flow to each and all. May the Divine bring clarity, healing and restitution in the most appropriate ways. May love, clarity, wholeness and blessing, flow to each and all."

Thank you, Divine Ones, thank you Streams of Consciousness for the wisdom and revelations.
I honor my knowing and I honor the sacred now and my being.
I am in appreciation and recognition to integrate these blessings in my being and my life.

In this moment, I move into a space of my wholeness.
Thank you. Thank you. Thank you.

Take another slow, deep breath. Center yourself.
And so it is.
And so it shall be.

Now you may think about, journal and reflect upon the insights, wisdom and transformations you received and perceived.

PART 4

Inspiration

Opening the Way

CHAPTER TWENTY:

Engaging The Streams

T he Streams of Consciousness have now been revealed. The mysteries are now open for your exploration, experience, awakening and so much more.

Dear Children of Earth, blessed beings of Gaia Terra,
You have received the trails of energy that do lead to direct access to the Divine and also to ways of communicating, being and sharing the Divine in yourself and in this world.

We know you are spiritual beings who have chosen to live on Gaia Terra at this time. Now, we have unveiled the mysteries of these Streams of Consciousness, so you may have direct access and also understand ways to participate.

Take this moment and breathe and acknowledge your own journey to this moment.

Many lifetimes, many relationships and many pathways have led you here. Now, you have met and experienced initial contact with the Streams of Consciousness that have flowed and influenced your world since the ancient times. How you interact, how you respond and how you share this elegant, sacred and ever expanding energy is now an opening for evolution, transformation, healing, blessing and sacred realignment. Reading each chapter is an introduction to the individual Streams of Consciousness. Most likely, you have made an initial connection with each stream and have felt the brilliance therein.

Initial Encounters

As you encountered each Stream of Consciousness, were some of them familiar to you? Did you feel a deeper connection with a specific Stream of Consciousness? Did it awaken memories or feel like it is part of you? Did you feel a resonance, an alignment with a specific stream and know that you want to continue connecting with that trail?

This specific Stream of Consciousness may be your aligning stream. You may have a deep connection with this energy in this lifetime. You may have encountered and resonated to this specific Stream of Consciousness many times, but you were unaware and therefore could not access it directly. It may have a true familiarity that you love. You may have aligned with this specific stream in other lifetimes and called it other names. Even now, this stream may indeed be aligned with you and you recognize part of it, and now you can experience the greater fullness. This may be the Stream of Consciousness that calls you into your greater being. It may be the stream that inspires awakenings and new perspectives and opportunities to shine in this life. Each and every Stream of Consciousness has inspired and influenced many individuals, many groups, many cultures and societies on this planet.

As you encountered each Stream of Consciousness, reading about their energies and influence and experiencing some of those awakening vibrations, did you discover some streams that you want to explore? Did you find inspiration and intrigue that seems to call you? A Stream of Consciousness may call to you so you can experience something magickal about that energy and wisdom. It may open a knowing, even when you know it may not be your path of expression. You may have friends or a community that you feel is aligned with this Stream of Consciousness. You may feel the influence of this stream in your life and our world. The Streams of Consciousness have inspired groups and collectives and cultures. You may feel that connection. If that does occur to you, follow the inquiry and vibration. You may be delighted with hidden wisdom that can evolutionize your thinking and being.

Were you illuminated by a Stream of Consciousness? Did you receive that burst of light, that awakening feeling, that acceleration of consciousness? Did you receive immediate inspiration and knowing? Was there an infusion of energy that shifted your perspective? Did you lose track of time or feel multi-dimensional in your own being? You may have been illuminated by a Stream of Consciousness. When this happens there is a higher level of experience which can be immediately transformative. The word enlightenment has been used to describe this connection when higher frequencies combine with greater wisdom and an awakening consciousness occurs. If this is so for you, beautiful! Honor your journey and do what you need and what is best to integrate the energies into your own knowing and being.

Consciously Engaging the Streams

Now that you have been introduced to these trails, I shall suggest different ways to engage the Streams of Consciousness, so you may bring those alignments forward in your life, and therefore in this world. Now, that you have been introduced to the Streams of Consciousness, you can access them. This is your private and personal relationship which always gives direct access to the Divine.

First, it is beneficial to have a centering and sacred practice to enter the Streams of Consciousness. You may have your own sacred rituals and practices that create the clear vibrational space that holds a centered, focused and spiritual compass for your connections. If you do, then I, Alawashka, suggest that you do your practices when you engage the Streams of Consciousness. This creates a clarity and a sacredness that serves these highest frequencies and serves you, as well.

If you do not have your own discipline or ceremony, then please do The Alawashka Chant of Blessing Practice that we included in this book for you. The Chant of Blessing Practice is very clear and will naturally align you to your higher vibrations of being. It will create the personal sacred space that will be a container for these frequencies and for your own energy, so you are held, embraced, honored and safe.

Conscious Connection with the Streams

Now, in sacred space, you are ready to engage the Streams of Consciousness in a more conscious connection. As we mentioned earlier, open to these energies within the sacred, honor yourself and your own journey, honor all beings, all life in your connection with the Divine and the Streams of Consciousness. This is the first practice. Create the sacred space for your own encounters. Each time you encounter, consciously connect with and enter the Streams of Consciousness, do your sacred practice to honor the stream and to honor yourself.

In your first conscious connection with an individual Stream of Consciousness, look to your heart and your inner guidance to select the one stream that feels most appropriate to you at that moment. When you choose the stream that calls you and you feel a kindred connection, you are listening to yourself and listening to the stream. This may not be your only choice of stream. It is the stream that feels right, that feels resonant and connected and compatible to you. That is the stream you can choose first. Why? In a way it is beckoning to you. There are gifts within for you to receive. There are insights and answers for you to understand. This stream may hold your next attunements. It may hold a deepening for your being and the endless flow and wisdom you seek.

There may even be resolution of quandaries you have in this life or from other times. You may discover your ancient heritage, your soul family, your off-world brothers, your divine guides and more. Follow the invitation from your own being and from the individual Stream of Consciousness for your first conscious connection.

Explore the beauty and wisdom of this specifically chosen Stream of Consciousness. Take your time. Honor and harmonize with the energies – your energy and the energies of the stream. There is no need to rush. You may discover that this particular stream is home, that you have waited for this invitation into this sacred realm. Allow yourself that gift. If you want to explore other streams too, that is open to you at all times. Your choice of one stream in this moment does not isolate you from other streams. In truth, you may comprehend, awaken and know the other streams through this stream you have chosen. We shall talk about this, too.

When you feel it is time to explore another Stream of Consciousness, ask yourself and the wisdom of the stream, if there is anything else at this time that is beneficial for you to know, experience and receive from this stream. If the answer is yes, then reach toward that matrix and see if it is right for you, now. If yes, then stay until you feel complete for the time being. It is more beneficial to receive the frequencies while you are already in alignment with that stream in the present, than to enter again and move into resonance.

Take time to digest and infuse the wisdom, frequencies and transformations you receive. There is so much within each Stream of Consciousness, that you want to be in harmony with those gifts. Lumari is very aligned with writing and she journals and writes. We suggest that you find the most complementary way to note, record and document your own journey. This will hold insights that you may reflect back upon and wisdom that you may not be ready to infuse in the moment, but is still present in your being.

When you are ready to encounter another Stream of Consciousness, be open to how you chose. Sometimes the Stream of Consciousness chooses you. It calls to you and you move towards it, knowing the resonance is true. Sometimes it is you, calling the Stream of Consciousness. You feel a longing, a connection, an inquiry that this stream may best serve. Either way, as you open to that stream do The Chant of Blessing Practice or your own centering and sacred practice to set the space for your direct Divine connection.

Lumari and I will be expanding the resonance and vibrations of the Stream of Consciousness, to include personal attunements and group participation events. You may contact Lumari to participate. Personal attunements harmonize you with your relationships with the Streams. Group participation with the Streams of Consciousness is more rich and complex, given the energies of each person in the collective of beings. We do want you to know this will be forthcoming. First, it was important to reveal the mysteries and introduce the Streams of Consciousness. Now, we will include group participation.

Blessings

May the blessings you receive
from the Streams of Consciousness
bring gifts that expand your knowing,
bless your life, create healing and celebrate
your own path of beauty.

CHAPTER TWENTY ONE:

Influences of The Streams

The Streams of Consciousness are sending their elegant and inspirational energies to this planet at all times. Their energies, their qualities have been the inspiration for the highest and most lofty endeavors of humanity. The qualities and resonances of each stream move to special rhythms that provide guidance and connection to the Divine. As more and more people experience the effects of the Streams of Consciousness, the qualities of the streams become distinctions that a person can incorporate in their life. This may happen whether you are working within the resonance of a specific stream, whether the energies of that stream have influenced the community in which you participate, or whether you are illuminated by the stream.

Once the frequencies of illumination from the Stream of Consciousness touch a person, then begins the work of bringing that resonance into the world. Each person will have a different talent or guidance for the expression of that illumination. Their life and gifts will reflect the illumination. Many people have experienced the flows of illumination from a Stream of Consciousness. Many leaders in the arts, in social, economic, spiritual and agricultural arenas have been illuminated by a particular stream and have dedicated their lives and contributed to changes that uplift and transform your world through their personally augmented view.

Many people have been so moved and inspired by the illumination within a Stream of Consciousness that they have dedicated their lives toward transforming the world through their personally augmented view. Yet each has transformed the world and the way we perceive the world from their own inspired perspective and gifts. There are no criteria in the Streams of Consciousness that a person act a certain way or be holy and above the pulses of humanity. The illumination provides the pathways to reach the height of being human, not avoiding it. Every person and being who is illuminated by the vibrations, patterns and qualities of a Stream of Consciousness proceeds from that experience in harmony with their own gifts.

Life and spiritual experiences have been guided by the qualities and participation of the Streams of Consciousness. Times of historical and cultural growth have been inspired by contact with a stream and the qualities of Divine resonance within that stream.

It is not necessary to become illuminated by a Stream of Consciousness to resonate with and embrace the flows of their pathways. You do not need to be illuminated by a stream to receive the bounty and connection of Divine participation. People have always chosen to flow in resonance with their own personal alignment. The Divine moves through everything at all times. The Streams of Consciousness are accelerated, concentrated and expedient avenues for spiritual upliftment, awakening and participation. While not all changes have come about because of affiliation with or influence by a Stream of Consciousness, the most transformational changes on this planet that have affected large populations and cultures have evolved through this gracious encounter.

Historically, there have been times when the illumination of one person has changed the tempo and course of human experience. This can be seen most by following the positive influences of art, spirituality and social relatedness. At times, a small community has embraced and worked with the qualities of one stream and then altered human perceptions through their own experiences. Other times, the influences of one or several Streams of Consciousness have set off a chain of spiritual and societal inspirations that have affected life around the globe. The resonance of the Streams of Consciousness, whether through an individual influence or in a collaborative influence, provide a greatly expanded, highly refined and gracefully attuned spiritual experience. This is the stream's matrix and vibrational alignment and purpose. The Streams of Consciousness were created as a gift to humanity to expand awareness and contribute the highest qualities of Divine recognition. With this book, they are revealed so you may recognize the blessings that have showered upon this planet since ancient times.

The Relationships of the Streams of Consciousness

The Streams of Consciousness have inspired humanity's joyous leaps into greater awakening, understanding and transformation. They have provided clear pathways to Divine encounters and experiences. All streams work the same way, although they do not have the same attunements. Each stream has its own relationship or thematic energy coding which conveys an aspect of Divine essence. In truth, Divine essence is only conveyed in aspects and not totality. No one being can experience the totality of the Divine. Specifically, it is a scientific impossibility. Yet, each being and person holds the truth of the Divine as a microcosm within them, and therefore, the above sentence is contradicted. Of course, experience of and translation of are two very different things.

Each Stream of Consciousness moves in highly specific ways and triggers certain energies and patterns. The individuals and cultures who resonate to a specific stream do so because their energy is in complementary compatibility to how wisdom or experience is received or retrieved. Similar information or spiritual resources may be accessed by different streams, although the feeling or experience of the deep knowing will be different. The resonance of the stream is different and accessing the "information" is different.

Each of the individual Streams of Consciousness follows their specific patterns of organization, so that travelers within the stream will, firstly, be aware of the stream and its nature and, secondly, be more able to access the vibrational patterns and attunements for spiritual expansion and growth. Each of the individual Streams has its own innate wisdom.

Every Stream of Consciousness imparts or attunes Divine understanding. The nature of the Streams of Consciousness is to reach and activate an individual or group of individuals with spiritual energy and understanding so they may reach higher states of knowing and evolution. The attunement of the stream will guide an individual to greater knowing through its focus upon certain energies and qualities. The "result" of experiencing the energy of a particular Stream can be a greater and more profound understanding of Divinity and expansion. This understanding can appear to be the exact same "knowing" or "truth" as another, yet it is accessed by a very different path and through a very different relationship to the energy.

This difference is highly unique in its format and expression. The differences among and between the Streams of Consciousness reveal twelve dominant energy attunements that provide a collective human experience. Each Stream of Consciousness holds a resonance of and to the vibratory patterns that will sustain that quality and energy. Each Stream is a revelation of and pathway to Divine connection and consciousness. When a person, group or culture is in resonance with, in relationship with a Stream of Consciousness, they appreciate and value its expression in every moment of everyday life. They live their lives attuned to that particular stream and focus, and they know or intuit that this pathway to Divine revelation and life is most aligned with their own being.

What is also brilliant and unique for you is that by knowing each Stream of Consciousness and understanding the energies, resonance and experience within that Stream, you can begin to more fully understand the individual or group or culture that is aligned with that Stream and its pathway to spirit and to understanding their life view. You gain a richer connection with your own resonant perspective and can more fully understand and appreciate the individuals, groups, cultures and societies in your world today.

The Distinction of Different Streams of Consciousness

Distinguishing the differences among the Streams of Consciousness may sometimes be subtle. The direction and revelation may appear to be the same, and yet the pathway is different. To help you see and appreciate these differences, this example will describe the distinctions of two different Streams of Consciousness, the Stream of Harmony and the Stream of Wisdom. Through each stream an individual can experience and know the interrelatedness of all life. By direct experience this individual can feel how each part of life, whether it is nature or human made, all appears to fit together and impress itself upon every aspect of life. Through this understanding, an individual can feel and understand how their life does affect and can uplift everyone and everything. This knowing is assured by both the Stream of Harmony and the Stream of Wisdom. The difference in this example is that the way this knowing is felt and experienced is directed by the focus of the stream itself. The individual and group's life experience will be influenced by the focus and quality of the stream, even if the knowing itself is similar.

The Stream of Harmony resonates with a fullness, a collective and collaborative energy to support and reveal the blessings it imparts. Each individual experience in this stream gives voice to the wholeness of the Stream of Harmony. It focuses, expresses and reveals through interrelatedness, many parts interconnected creating a whole. Spiritual knowing and perception is guided and directed by the experience of harmony. The Stream of Harmony magnifies life as an interrelated system of compatible symmetry, and one's view of life will converge from this perception.

The Stream of Wisdom resonates with an expression of Divine continuity, reverberating ancient wisdom through rhythmic associations. Each individual would experience life and Divine knowing through the rhythmic cycles of wisdom that span the Divine. Spiritual knowing and perception is guided and directed by the experience of ancient rhythms of knowing. The Stream of Wisdom correlates life as an interrelated flow of rhythmic associations and interconnections through the ages, and one's view of life will expand from this perception.

The vibrational make-up of the Stream of Harmony appears to be in a 'present now.' The vibrational patterns collaborate and intertwine as each particulate is expressed. Its vibratory patterns move in kaleidoscopic events, in the moment. Therefore, one could view the Stream of Harmony as cohesive bursts and flow, reverberating in the moment and echoing through time to illuminate the brilliant interrelatedness of the Divine.

The vibrational make-up of the Stream of Wisdom appears to be a longer matrix. The vibrational pattern extends outward and is more durational. Its vibratory patterns move in longer strokes throughout time. Therefore, one could view the Stream of Wisdom as waves within the great cycle of knowing, reverberating through time and space to illuminate the brilliant interconnections of the Divine.

Participating with the Stream of Wisdom, an individual can move in rhythmic expression of Divine knowing.

The cycle and pulse of this energy brings new avenues for spiritual awareness and awakening. It brings ancient wisdom through time and contributes to contemporary thought. It vibrates into an expression of the Divine that expounds continuity. The Stream of Wisdom spans the ages and illuminates the cycles. When cycles are illuminated, they are rhythms. They can be followed and emulated. Knowing the rhythm, one can learn to participate within and create that rhythm. Therein lies the sacred and the access to the Divine.

An individual who feels most akin with the melodies of spirit would resonate to the Stream of Harmony. Just as in a musical group, their preferred instrument would be able to produce melody and song. The individual who thrives with rhythms would prefer instruments of a more percussive nature. Sometimes one may notice Harmony above Rhythm. Sometimes one may notice Rhythm above Harmony. Each is present. Each Stream of Consciousness contributes to the whole. The Stream of Harmony reveals and creates a direct connection with the Divine through a clear awareness and experience that each being, each thought, contributes to the wholeness. Each person, each energy creates the collective, comprised of brilliant individual aspects, creating a harmony of life and the Divine. The Stream of Wisdom reveals and creates a direct connection with the Divine through collecting, recognizing and infusing the brilliance of the Divine throughout time. The ancient knowing of all peoples, of all cultures, flows and infuses life, to bless, influence and create the present knowing. Each person, each energy, follows, flows with and creates a sacred rhythm of wisdom and connection with the Divine. By understanding which Stream of Consciousness an individual prefers or resonates to, one can have a deeper understanding and appreciation of that individual. This appreciation and understanding can extend to the culture or society that is influenced and participates with each stream.

The feelings, experiences and energies of each Stream of Consciousness are very different, even if the outcome or inspiration is the same. In comparing these two streams, the Stream of Harmony would be an experience of all of the voices through time who sing the melodies of knowing. The Stream of Wisdom would be an experience of all of the ancient rhythms which bind the melodies into a collaborative wholeness. The Stream of Harmony may attract people who are aligned with and celebrate how each person comes together in the now, to create Divine connection. The Stream of Wisdom may attract people who are aligned with the flow of sacred wisdom and attunements throughout time, honoring the ancient teachings and timeless wisdom, and infusing their lives with those rhythms of life pulsing throughout this world.

Using deep understanding, each person would experience and know the interrelatedness of all life and experience a direct connection with the Divine and yet, each would feel their own unique individual life differently in resonance with each Stream of Consciousness. This view, this comparison, gives you an opportunity to appreciate the distinct alignments, perspectives and perceptions of individuals and groups and societies, through their resonance and relationships with the individual Stream of Consciousness. It opens you to see yourself in relationship with others, in relationship with other Streams of Consciousness and to appreciate the different experiences and expressions that celebrate the Divine.

CHAPTER TWENTY TWO:

The New Illuminated Paradigm

This is a new moment, a new day, a new awakening. This is the time for the new paradigm and a new future. We declare this to be so.

The new illuminated paradigm is a new experience and creation of how the world and your participation in it unfolds. It is a new future. It is not based on the past, on the cumulative effects and results of what has gone before you. Creating a new paradigm is creating a world, a reality based on what you want to experience and know can be experienced. You create a new paradigm by bringing your fullness and aspirations into a higher level of reality. Your deeper understanding of community, relatedness, fulfillment, joy, appreciation and continuity will create a new reality if you choose to make it so. The dreams and aspirations of your life are opening for fulfillment in this moment.

This book is written to reveal the Streams of Consciousness to you, so you can clearly see how life on this dear planet has evolved through access to these streams. This book is written to help you distinguish the nature and qualities of all of the streams, so you may better understand the cultures and peoples of this world. To create a global community of fulfillment and upliftment, it serves you to understand and distinguish the threads of spiritual perception that are flowing. By revealing the vibrational pathways and sacred teachings of the Streams of Consciousness, we provide you with the opportunity to deepen your understanding and appreciation of human evolution up to this moment. You now have the opportunity to participate in expanded ways.

The Streams of Consciousness are openings, portals and streams of Divine energy that resonate with clear, direct connections with the Divine. Each Stream of Consciousness has very special qualities, and the combination of these qualities continue to resonate with and provide the spiritual and vibrational platform to help uplift humanity and this world. Each Stream, on its own and in combination with the others, creates a dynamic spiritual resonance to invite and generate gracious expansions and awakenings for higher perception. Each of the twelve Streams of Consciousness, when resonating in harmony, can bring a new spiritual relatedness to your life and to the lives of every being on this planet, human, animal, plant, mineral and ethereal. Feel into this wisdom. Attentively imagine each Stream's qualities augmenting the others, so that all are vibrating in a harmonious celebration of life.

Each Stream can teach you about the awareness and impetus of those resonating to it. Each Stream of Consciousness has a view, an attunement through which those resonating to it perceive their world. Knowing this attunement and knowing the higher vibrational levels of those attunements, you can truly appreciate the blessings that people who are aligned with those frequencies can contribute to your world.

To bring this world, this moment, into the new illuminated paradigm, you perceive what the past has generated and then bring the highest energies into play.

Imagine the gifts of every Stream of Consciousness in their full capacity. Every one, every Stream can bring blessing and enlightenment. Every quality is an enormous gift. What would happen if, by knowing and presencing the clear vibrations within the Streams of Consciousness, you could bring the higher energies into play?

Shifting Awareness

To create a new illuminated paradigm, is to own and honor the past, while moving into a new way of being. To own and honor the past, one acknowledges the brilliance, the awakenings and evolution and contribution from the past. To own and honor the past, one acknowledges the wrongdoings that have transpired. Then through that truth, through that level of integrity, one moves into the future to create a greater harmony. By moving into a deeper understanding of the blessings and gifts from the Streams of Consciousness, you can recognize the gifts and the triggers that will bring a new awakening into blossom.

When you understand the qualities and flows of the Stream of Honor, for example, you can begin to understand the triggers that people resonating to this Stream may encounter. They may become alarmed or resistant to anyone or anything that creates a feeling of disrespect for them, their family, their way of life. When you understand the qualities that move within the Stream of Neutrality, for example, you can begin to understand how a person resonating to that energy may respond to a situation which requires a quick decision when little of the information is yet known. If one is resonating to Neutrality, how does one proceed without enough information to make a competent yet personally unbiased decision? When you understand the qualities that resonate in the Stream of Wisdom, you can begin to understand the powers of memory. If you are trying to create something new with someone resonating from the Stream of Wisdom, their timing and flow may feel slower to someone who does not appreciate the breadth of their personal scope, memory and vision.

When you understand the energies and qualities of each Stream of Consciousness, and you view the world with the perspective of each stream's sphere of influence, you can understand how a person, group or culture feels. You can understand why they feel that way, because you can understand and perceive the Stream of Consciousness that inspired their ways of life. As each stream has a specific resonance and influence across most of the world. By exploring the different streams, their spiritual qualities and regions of influence, you can look at areas of the globe or specific populations and begin to understand why they live their lives a certain way. You can begin to understand what they react to or embrace. You can begin to perceive their point of reference and by doing so, approach them from within that reference and resonance. You can then move into honor and harmony with them to create the many bridges necessary to bring a high level of relatedness and appreciation into the world.

When you understand the energies and qualities of each Stream of Consciousness, you may also have a greater understanding of how and why many people may view your world in different ways. People illuminated by and resonating with a Stream of Consciousness may interpret life, people, relationships, the planet and each other, through the focus of that stream. The unknown and untold existence of the Streams of Consciousness is revealed and written for your awakening and to gift you with more opportunities to shift your awareness, activate new perspectives and healing, and uplift your world into the new, higher paradigms that you long to express and live. In this revelation, we also ask that you let go of the limited thinking and judgments that can accompany this understanding. You may resonate with one Stream of Consciousness, and that may give you a brilliant perspective. And yet, you may have judgments or opinions or even distain for another way of resonating, thinking or being.

When humanity began to devise interpretations of a Stream of Consciousness, then the resonance became narrow.

Experiences became interpretations. Interpretations became ideology. Ideology became practices, and practices became rules. Although these human interpretations were initially formulated and constructed to help people move within a Stream of Consciousness and understand the richness of the vibrations, they also became solidified ways of thinking and being. Individuals, societies, cultures, religions and geographic locations formulated ways of being, thinking and behaving that not only generated opportunities to experience a Stream of Consciousness, but also became preferences and more limited ways of viewing life, spirit and each other. Preference of one Stream of Consciousness became a way of life. Preference of one Stream of Consciousness also became an evaluation about other ways of being and living. This process of developing ideology, practices and rules became assessment, opinion and a source of distinction that also became a means of separation.

Now, knowing this too, you have the opportunity to shift into resonance with the Stream of Consciousness that expands your being and knowing and move into a new synchronicity with the Divine and the Divine in you. Now Life is open for reorientation.

The Streams of Consciousness were originally created to give humanity clear, direct connections with the Divine. This was to help those individuals who were overwhelmed in the immensity of the Singular Outpouring and truly wanted their personal connection and relationship with the Divine. The Streams of Consciousness were created to shine a light and bring the highest frequencies of direct, Divine connection in clarity, blessing, expansion and profound knowing. Each Stream of Consciousness was created for this world with very special qualities, because the individual qualities and the combination of these qualities would and do provide the spiritual and vibrational platform to help uplift humanity and this world. Each quality, on its own and in combination with the others, creates a dynamic spiritual resonance that generates the gracious expansion and awakening needed for higher perception.

We reveal the Streams of Consciousness now, so that each person, to your own degree, have the opportunity and clarity to awaken the reverence and appreciation for your own life and everyone else's life. Each of you has the opportunity to know the profound understanding of your own relatedness to everything while being present to an expanded vision of centeredness.

You can know the intimate collaboration and harmony of creation, and feel the beauty and grace contained within all life. You can feel the wisdom pulsing through every aspect of consciousness, know the full clarity of the fundamental truth and joyously radiate that knowing in every direction. You can know that everything you do and everything you are responds and corresponds to all of creation. You can feel the thread of the Divine moving through every individual particle of creation and uniting every aspect of being. Through these resonances and through the qualities of the Streams of Consciousness, each person will grow to know that they can and you can create a life and a world filled with Divine inspiration, connection and recognition. You can indeed create a new illuminated paradigm.

This new illuminated paradigm is a vibrational undertaking in which humanity moves to a more appreciative and creative participation in the world. In this new illuminated paradigm, humanity moves to embrace their own individual spiritual connection in freedom and joy. Each person begins to contribute to the flow of creation, without the harsh judgment on life-style and belief. In the new illuminated paradigm, relatedness, appreciation, honor and fulfillment move in harmony with the spiritual and Divine flow of creation.

This is where your dreams come from, the knowing, guidance and belief that your lives can be filled with enrichment. The vibrational cohesion of a new illuminated paradigm travels through each and all of the Streams of Consciousness to awaken the deeper dreams of reality within you. As you long to create a world and a life filled with abundance and joy and fulfillment and honor, you are met by the Streams of Consciousness in this awakening.

By revealing that these streams are present, Lumari and I have awakened and opened a pathway of appreciation and connectivity for you. By knowing that the Streams of Consciousness are present, by understanding what qualities they embody and where they have engaged their energies, you can help to heal the past confusions of history, religion and preference. You can connect with people by honoring and recognizing their own wisdom. Then their wisdom can be a solid contribution to your life and your vision of the future.

Each Stream of Consciousness has gifts and blessings to impart. Through recognizing those energies you can meet those blessings. You can invite those gifts into your life through contact with the individual streams or through contact with people who are touched by those streams.

By discerning the energies that are available, by knowing and resonating to the Streams of Consciousness and by creating an opening wherein these beautiful energies can uplift and embrace your life, you will uplift your own awareness and the lives of others. You can begin to create a new illuminated paradigm flowing with Divine celebration. You can begin to create a world where honor, appreciation and fulfillment move gracefully in everyone's life.

In this moment, tune into your own experience. You participated in an intimate collaboration with creation. You have discovered, aligned with and are present to the Streams of Consciousness. Feel the beauty, grace, truth, awakening and healing joyously radiating in every direction.

All who are ready will receive and respond. Know that whether an individual knows at this moment, through these resonances and through the qualities of the Streams of Consciousness, each person will grow to know that they can create a life and a world filled with Divine inspiration, connection and recognition.

Now, we have revealed the Streams of Consciousness.
You have been on a very sacred revelation journey in this book.
The frequencies and wisdom are abounding and you are here.
Take several deep breaths. Allow the wisdom, knowledge and frequencies to flow and also to settle.
Be in a space of non-judgment and simple perception.

If you feel deep understanding and gratitude for these revelations, be in the space of gratitude.
If you feel confusion and uncertainty for these revelations, be in the space of honor and curiosity.
If you feel moved to understand the Streams of Consciousness more, do connect with Lumari for the teachings and groups she will bring.

Let us all breathe and create a space that is bigger and more open to wisdom.

This is what the Streams of Consciousness always present and provide.

Allow and encourage the vibrations, tunings and wisdom to flow.

Blessings

Now, you are a knowing part of the dream.
You are a knowing part of the blessings of life
and this world.

May this moment be a blessing for you
and for all beings,
from this moment on into the infinite, eternal, now.

May the gracious, sacred awakening shine.

You are part of these blessings.
And so it is.

About The Author

L UMARI is a gifted internationally acclaimed intuitive life coach, psychic consultant, creative catalyst, visionary energy master and bestselling author who has shown thousands of people how to celebrate their soul purpose, follow their highest destiny, fulfill their dreams and Live Inspired.

With clients all over the world, she is passionate about providing guidance and sharing wisdom that creates transformation, fulfillment and inspiration for positive personal, professional and planetary change.

Enjoying a successful career as a sculptor, Lumari integrated her creative gifts as an artist with her powerful intuitive gifts of vision, channeling and communication to relentlessly follow her vision. Because of her extraordinary intuitive gifts, vibration and wisdom, Lumari is a joyful vortex of inspiration. She opens the doors to your inner being. Her world class coaching provides the clarity, guidance and healing you need to fulfill your soul expression, soar in spirit, access opportunities and manifest greater wealth and success. Her insight, vibration and vision help you be the joyful soul and spirit you know you are inside and guide you to courageous success.

Her books, meditations and spiritual training workshops bring joyful awakening, profound clarity, spiritual connection and healing. They reveal secret teachings to raise awareness and Divine connection.

Her podcast the "Cosmic Coffee Break" brings enlightening meditations, wisdom teachings and interviews to share the vibrations to uplift your life and our world.

To connect with Lumari for coaching, gatherings and more and to Live Inspired, email Contact@Lumari.com

Books from Lumari

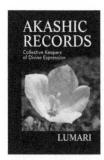

AKASHIC RECORDS

Learn about the Akashic Records and the Beings who hold the Wisdom of the Ages. Lumari is the first to interview and channel direct communication with the Akashic. Discover who the Akashic Records are, how their system of Universal wisdom works and how to achieve a connection of your own.

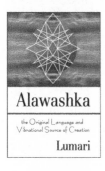

ALAWASHKA

Discover the nature of Creation, the evolution of humanity and the power of Alawashka, the original language of Creation. Channeled by Lumari, the words and energies in this book contain vibrations of universal transformation and can initiate your passage into higher consciousness, just by reading it.

LIVING INSPIRED WITH LUMARI

In this book, Lumari breaks apart the myths that rob you of the true vibrations of living inspired. She reveals the ART of Living Inspired, so you can create your own illumination and positive purpose every moment.

SHOPPING FOR A MAN

Find deeper personal fulfillment and create a lasting, meaningful relationship without playing games or sacrificing yourself. Lumari's wisdom teachings, visualizations and evolutionary shopping tips will help you date a fabulous guy who's the right fit for you.

More from Lumari

ACTIVATIONS JOURNAL

"Your Journal is your Journey" This journal is a powerful companion guide to the Streams Of Consciousness book. You will gain greater insights, healing and awakening as you create your direct, personal connection to the Divine. Download your free Activations Journal and more free gifts at CosmicStreams.com

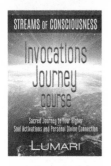

INVOCATIONS JOURNEY Course

Experience clear, harmonious resonance. The Streams of Consciousness Invocations audio course includes Sacred practices, Calling Forth the Streams chants, High Frequency meditations, Invocation Guide Book, and Invocations Journal.
Start your journey here ~ CosmicStreams.com

CLAIM YOUR SPIRITUAL REAL ESTATE

Keep your energy clear and protected, while you follow your destiny Course includes teachings and training to lift your spirit and place you right in the center of your own being, power and purpose, with energy to spare. Over 6 Hours of Audio Home Study Course Lumari.com

PERSONAL SACRED SPACE Meditation

Receive the essential secrets to stay clear and connected to your own energy vision and purpose, in your sacred space of being. Download free audio meditation ~ Lumari.com

Blessings

Blessings For You

May you receive and kow the blessings of your life
and your gifts.

May you celebrate with joy, love and clarity.

May the Streams of Consciousness Bless you.

As best serves you, your life and your soul's calling
May you receive blessings of
Purity, Honor, Compassion, Neutrality,
Harmony, Beauty and Grace,
Wisdom, Truth, Radiance, Reciprocity
Universality and Unity.

May you have more opportunities to Shine.

Made in the USA
Las Vegas, NV
07 April 2021